Steve Croft i... ...large, growing church in Halifax, and is Mission Consultant in the Diocese of Wakefield.

*Also available from Marshall Pickering
by the same author*

Growing New Christians

Making New Disciples

Steps to Christian Growth
a practical handbook

STEVE CROFT

HarperCollins
An Imprint of HarperCollins*Publishers*

Marshall Pickering is an Imprint of
HarperCollins*Religious*
Part of HarperCollins*Publishers*
77–85 Fulham Palace Road, London W6 8JB

First published in Great Britain
in 1994 by Marshall Pickering

1 3 5 7 9 10 8 6 4 2

A catalogue record for this book is
available from the British Library

ISBN 0 551 02862–9

Printed and bound in Great Britain by
HarperCollinsManufacturing Glasgow

Contents

Introduction

The challenge

Sitting near the back of church on a typical Sunday morning is a man in an untidy leather jacket listening hard to the sermon.

Brian is in his late twenties. His childhood was scarred by difficulties in his family. Throughout his adult life, Brian has moved from job to job. He has two children through different partners and has recently separated from a third. A few months ago, through the witness of a family member, Brian became a Christian. At the time and for a while afterwards, he was on the edge of a breakdown. Since coming to faith, Brian has developed good habits of worship. He's joined a group in the church for enquirers and new Christians and has been confirmed. He's also received a certain amount of counselling and practical help. Brian would be the first to say that he has a long way to go in his new Christian life.

A few pews in front of Brian sits Lesley, a young girl in her early twenties. She comes from a more stable family background but is the only committed Christian in her family. Lesley came to know Christ about eighteen months ago through a friend at school. In the next five to ten years, Lesley will pass through many changes in her life as she grows from young person to adult. Will her faith keep growing through the testing times ahead?

Near the front of church sits Angela with a friend. Angela, too, became a Christian a couple of years ago, this time through friendships in the parent and toddler group. Since that time she's been a member of a home group and has taken on a ministry within the church. But she's never really developed a discipline of Sunday worship – mainly due to pressures at home. Her commitment to Christ rises and falls with the seasons. Several times now there has been a real danger that she would drift away altogether. How can the rest of the church family help her to grow?

Across the aisle is George, an older man. George has lived on his own since his wife died last year. In the midst of his grief he has found a real faith. Will that faith continue to grow and flourish over the next few years or quietly die away – perhaps leaving a habit of church attendance but no inner reality?

These are four people of different ages and backgrounds all new to the Christian faith. There are others like them in our own church and in thousands of other churches throughout the country. The challenge to every church is to understand how to bring these new Christians to maturity and to put that understanding into practise. This book is an attempt to help that process.

Aiming for the wrong target

When we set goals in our evangelism we often aim too low. We are content, sometimes, when a person simply begins attending church where there has been no sharing in worship before. There are perhaps good grounds for being encouraged. The congregation has grown by one. Surely the person will be receiving something from worship.

Yet persuading people to come to church regularly is too small a vision of evangelism. Those people also need to come to know God for themselves through Christ and be filled with the Holy Spirit. That will happen in a variety of ways. Understanding and responding to people's journey into faith is the theme of my earlier book, *Growing New Christians*.[1]

It is a very wonderful thing when a person is converted. There can be great joy and initial enthusiasm for Christ and the church. It can be a time of great learning and of the whole of life opening up in new ways.

Yet if our aim is to win converts to Christ, it is still not high enough. A church which is full of converts will not be able to fulfil its mission to transform the world. Nor will that church be able to grow beyond a certain point. Its members will remain spiritual children and will continue to make high demands of those who lead them to Christ instead of being able to fend for themselves and to minister to others as mature Christians. In that way they will take up all available energy and stifle growth.

Our aim must be to make more than attenders or converts but to make disciples – the commission Jesus gives us. To be a disciple means to be committed to grow and to develop and learn and mature and minister for God in whatever he asks you to do. A church full of disciples is able to have an impact on the world around us and is able to continue to grow in numbers and depth of fellowship.

A church full of dependant converts becomes a progressive drain on the demands of leadership. So much energy is expended on 'pastoral care' which consists of merely holding on to people and keeping them within the church structure. A church full of disciples is demanding to lead for different reasons: its members are constantly seeking God's will and his way and seeking new ways both to learn and to serve. If our evangelism is to have a lasting effect on church and nation then our aim has to be much more than increasing church attendance or numbers of conversions. We must become proficient at making disciples.

How to use this book

Making New Disciples comes in two parts. Part One looks at principles of Christian discipleship: key stages of growth; what we mean by 'Christian maturity' and what opposition we face. Part Two is a manual for helping Christians develop to maturity in eight different areas of the Christian life. As with *Growing New Christians*, the raw material for the book is my own experience of being vicar of St George's Church in Halifax.

A study guide has been provided for each chapter of the book, which is divided into four tracks for different readers:

Track One is for ministers and lay leaders. The track contains brief questions and exercises to help you think about your own situation with others in a staff team, ideas for sermons or training courses arising out of the chapter and, sometimes, ideas for further reading.

Track Two is for leaders of home groups or discipleship groups using all or part of the book as the basis for a course on Christian discipleship. Track 2 provides an outline group session for teaching the material in the preceding chapter including some group exercises, Bible studies, etc. For ideas on planning a group meeting and the way groups work please refer to the relevant chapters in *Growing New Christians*.[2]

Track Three is for those working through the material in the book on a one-to-one basis with a new Christian. What is envisaged here is a weekly or fortnightly meeting. Questions are provided in Track Three for discussion and conversation about applying what is written to individual lives. The track also gives Bible passages for further study.

Track Four is for those working through the book on their own either because you are a newish Christian yourself or because you feel you need to go back over some old ground. For this, I have envisaged your reading a chapter over a week or a fortnight, possibly keeping some kind of journal as you read. Bible passages are provided for daily reading. While you are working through the book I suggest you find time once a week for a longer time of prayer and reflection and various exercises are provided for this.

I would like to thank all those who have contributed ideas and suggestions particularly Ann, my wife, who has piloted the studies in the home group she leads; lay and ordained colleagues in Wakefield Diocese and the whole congregation at St George's, especially those who have kept on pointing out to me areas where they need to learn and to grow. This book has been much more challenging to write than its older sister. My own shortcomings have been very apparent to me as I have been writing it – yet so has the need for reflection and resources in this area of church life. The ideas are offered to the wider church in the hope that they will be useful in equipping the saints for the work of ministry.

Steve Croft

NOTES

1 Published by CPAS/Marshall Pickering, 1992.
2 Copies of the course handouts based on these chapters and written for St George's are available by post from St George's House, Lee Mount, Halifax, HX3 5BT at a cost of £5 for the basic pack and £15 for a licence to copy the handouts.

Part One

Principles of Christian Discipleship

one

Key Stages of Christian Growth

We proclaim Christ, admonishing and teaching everyone with all wisdom, so that we may present everyone perfect in Christ. To this end I labour, struggling with all his energy which so powerfully works in me.
Colossians 1.28

Four pictures of the way we grow

If our aim is to build mature disciples – not just to fill the church with converts – we need a clear idea of what we mean by Christian maturity. No builder will set to work without a plan provided and drawn up by the architect. We need to have a good understanding of what God intends the end result to be so that we can build with him. How does the Bible define maturity?

The Scriptures do not give one simple definition either of Christian maturity or the process of growing. Our starting point needs to be an understanding of the four great pictures the Bible uses for describing the process of Christian growth. They are the pictures of the journey, of agriculture, of building and of personal growth.

The journey

Stories of journeys abound in the Bible and in Christian literature. From the point of view of Christian growth the two most important journeys in the Bible are the story of the Exodus and the gospel accounts of the disciples' journey with Jesus during his ministry. Both were extended experiences of learning.

In Exodus the Israelites begin the journey as a frightened and divided group of former slaves uncertain of their identity and with only a doubtful commitment to their God who has saved them and to each other. By the end of the journey this group of slaves has become a well ordered nation with a clear ethical and religious code which was to sustain them for thousands of years; a nation able to shape the world in which it found itself. Along the journey in the wilderness there are lessons learned about God's provision, about his nature, his ways and his calling.

In the gospels, Jesus' disciples begin with an uncertain understanding of who he is and what he intends. They travel and watch, listen and question, put into practice and reflect on that practice. There are times of involvement and action and opportunities for rest and reflection. At the end of the journey the loose group of followers has become a highly motivated and committed group of disciples able to found the Church in the power of the Spirit and lay the seeds for the conversion of the Roman Empire.

These journeys, and others like them in the Scriptures, have lessons to teach us about Christian maturity. Growth is like a journey. It will continue for the rest of our lives. The paradox of Christian growth is that our aim is to become poor in spirit (Matthew 5:3). The more we know that we do not know, the greater our maturity in the faith. In all our teaching of discipleship this truth needs to be at the foundation: we never arrive. Any course of teaching which works on this idea of 'arrival' at maturity should be rejected. This is not the way God designed the Christian life. The nearer to God we travel the more we realize we have further to go. The goal of the journey is to become a better pilgrim.

The journey picture also teaches us important lessons about those who help along the way. Each Christian needs as principal guide the Holy Spirit, the one who walks alongside. Yet we all need human helpers and guides to point the way; to give assistance in time of difficulty; to keep us moving when we would rather stop and rest. Friends, family, our home group leader or the minister can all fulfil this role.

The model of the journey gives us a picture of the mature Christian not as one who has arrived, but as the seasoned traveller; with eyes firmly fixed on Jesus; prepared to learn new things as the road unfolds. Christian growth emerges as a dynamic interaction between the pilgrim Christian, the events of the journey and Christ himself, with friends and guides intervening from time to time.

Growing corn and fruit

In the Old Testament, the nation's spiritual life is often described in terms of vines, olives or some other crop growing and bearing fruit.[1] These pictures are developed by Jesus and applied to individual Christians in the parables of the kingdom[2] and in his teaching about the vine.[3] They are taken up by Paul in his description of evangelism and nurture and the work of the Holy Spirit in our lives.[4]

The goal of the process of growth in this second picture is fruitfulness. The farmer looks for good grapes from his vineyard and a mighty crop from his wheat field. The fruit is seen both as the extension of God's kingdom and as the developing of Christian qualities in our lives. To grow and bear this kind of fruit means radical change.

In this picture, Christian growth is clearly a gentle organic process which takes time. It cannot be forced or hurried. There will be significant moments in the course of that growing (weeding, watering, pruning and harvest) but most of the work of coming to maturity is hidden from sight. The pastor and Christian friend is involved at different points of the process as a farmer: planting, watering and weeding. But the pastor's work is not to make things happen. The pastor works in step with the Holy Spirit. As Paul writes, it is God who makes things grow. Those engaged in pastoral ministry are his fellow workers (1 Corinthians 3:8–9).

How much time does growing to fruitfulness take for a Christian? Different plants and crops have different maturation times – so do Christians. However, Jesus spent three years with his disciples patiently bringing them to maturity and watching good things beginning to grow in them. There was some fruit in those three years both in terms of personal qualities and the mission of the disciples, but the main ministry was to come later.

Does this mean then that in this picture at least we have an end point for maturity and Christian growth – the point at which the new Christian begins to bear fruit both in personal qualities or the building of the kingdom? The 'field' pictures give that impression. We need to set them alongside the great picture of the vine in John 15. We are branches of the vine, grafted into the stock. Life and growth come only from being rooted in the vine. The Father is the gardener. 'He cuts off every branch in me that bears no fruit, while every branch that does bear fruit he prunes so that it will be even more fruitful.' Like the seed which does not come to maturity in the sower parable, we see the process happening in all our churches. But for those who reach a degree of maturity and fruitfulness the dynamic of growth continues in the picture of pruning. We may pass through periods of great fruitfulness in our lives in terms of both personal growth and what we do. Jesus tells us clearly that in and after those times we will experience a pruning at God's hands. When the branch of a real vine is cut back, it is pruned to within a few inches of the stock and 'rests'. The following season it grows out and once again bears a rich harvest.

We should not then expect to be able to draw a graph of Christian growth which is a 'growth line' of fruitfulness: the longer we have been a Christian the more fruitful we become. Instead, like the vine, our fruit will be seasonal and periods of great fruitfulness will alternate with periods of cutting back and renewal. As we become older as Christians those periods of fruitfulness may become longer and more productive. The 'pruning' may also be deeper and longer. We cannot expect to evade the dry times.

As God's fellow workers and co-pastors we need to be alive to what he is doing not only in other people's lives but also in our own. We need to be prepared to invest a great deal of time and energy in new Christians to bring them to a point of maturity and bearing fruit. But those in our churches who have been Christians a long time will also need our help and attention. The home group leader who has been giving out constantly for three or four years and whose group has entered a static period needs a period of pruning in ministry and rest in the vine before something new can emerge. The long-standing church warden who finds it impossible to worship and hard even to pray needs a season of reduced commitments to focus again on Jesus. This time needs to be used not for anguished discussions of the 'What are we doing wrong?' kind but for simply resting and abiding in Jesus. Part of Christian maturity is recognizing the seasons of fruitfulness and pruning in our own lives. Part of pastoral care is helping other Christians see and respond to that dynamic in their own walk with the Lord.

Building a temple

The picture of building also has Old Testament roots in the building of the tabernacle, the foundation of the temple and the pictures of the prophets.[5] The idea of building is one used by Jesus in his parables about foundations and about counting the cost of discipleship.[6] It underlies much of the New Testament language about being established in faith and building each other up in Christ. The picture of the Christian being like a temple built to God's glory is used by Paul[7] who follows his teaching on Christian growth being like agriculture to expound the picture of building.

The laying of the foundations is clearly key to the building process. By God's grace, Paul has laid the foundation as the expert builder. Others are now building on this foundation but each should build with great care. Different builders are involved using a wide range of materials. The quality of each builder's work will be exposed on the day of judgement.

It is clear from 1 Corinthians 3 that, while a number of different builders may be at work, the chief builder once the foundations have been laid is the person themselves. Paul would be concerned therefore, as master builder, not only to lay a foundation but to teach each person how to go on building with God. Once that has happened, the chief responsibility for Christian growth and maturity rests not with the pastor or the church but with each individual Christian.

All too often when a Christian begins to stagnate the blame is laid at the door of the church. 'It's because of the preaching/worship/lack of fellowship here that I am not growing in my Christian life.' Clearly the church does play an important part in growth. But Paul would rebuke that attitude. Each individual Christian needs to be equipped to build and to oversee the building work within their own lives, not simply blame the contractor if the job is not proceeding to time. Again the Bible moves us away from a passive model of Christian growth which is simply to do with being in church or taking in teaching and gives us a dynamic picture of building involving God himself, the individual Christian and the wider church. The first two stages of the process are the laying of the foundations by the master builder and learning how to build for yourself. So much of what is done in terms of Christian growth in the church fosters dependence on 'pastors' and 'teachers'. The Bible teaches the exact opposite. Christians are to be taught to build for themselves.

The building picture is also used to emphasize that we grow in company with other Christians as part of the church. There are many other branches on the vine. Like living stones we are being built into a spiritual house. Although we are all individuals growing to maturity, we are also part of one body. Our growth is a corporate adventure. We affect each other. A Christian who joins a church full of other Christians growing and learning in the faith will grow much faster than one who is part of a church where the growth stopped for everyone soon after conversion. Although pastors may not bear primary responsibility for individual Christian lives, we have been given a solemn charge to ensure that our churches are places where Christians can grow and where maturity is taught and encouraged.

Is there an end to the building process? Certainly the building does reach a point where the foundations have been laid and it can proceed in rather a different way. We might think that it would not be many years before the building on site reached completion. But that would be because we have very little idea of what is involved in building a temple to God's glory. Solomon's temple took twenty years to build. As with one of the great cathedrals in our own country, even once the structure is finished and the basic furnishing installed the building work never comes to an end. There are repairs, restorations and improvements to be made. What was made with wood may need to be rebuilt in stone or inlaid with gold and silver. What was dedicated to God and made holy may become defiled and need to be cleansed. Parts may collapse putting the whole structure in danger. Just as on a visit to a great cathedral we will see masons and carpenters at work, so God's building of our lives into a temple of the Holy Spirit never comes to an end until we are with him.

Parenting a child

'When Israel was a child, I loved him and out of Egypt have I called my son.'[8]

Throughout the Old Testament, God is more than guide, gardener and builder. He is also Father. One of his concerns is to see his children grow to a mature, adult relationship with him.

The picture of God as Father and ourselves as his children is, of course, developed and deepened by Jesus who teaches us to call God Father. The word we are to use is 'Abba', the small child's personal form of address. We are to come to God as little children and remain in that childlike relationship with him. Yet at the same time we are called to grow to maturity.

For St Paul and the other apostles the whole business of evangelism and nurture is like having children and becoming a parent with all the pain, anxiety and joy that relationship demands.[9] Often in the New Testament letters the writers express a deep frustration that their readers have not yet grown up.[10]

The goal of growth, within this picture, is becoming an adult in faith. What does that mean? Clearly, as with the building work, some degree of independence is involved. A young child grows and develops from a situation of complete dependence upon his or her parents to a new relationship of interdependence in adult life. In the same way a new Christian needs to be growing from dependence upon pastors and teachers in the life of the church to independence.

Maturity is described in a striking picture in 1 Corinthians 13. In the midst of his description of Christian love Paul writes: 'When I was a child, I talked like a child, I thought like a child, I reasoned like a child. When I became a man, I put childish ways behind me.' Growing to maturity as a person and as a Christian means growing into love. A young child puts himself at the centre of the universe. As the child grows he learns gradually that he is not the centre and satisfying his needs is not the goal of every person around him. The core of love is the free self-giving of oneself to others – the love that Jesus demonstrates on the cross. Growing in that love is at the heart of becoming an adult in the Christian life.

Christians are called to be childlike but never childish. Growing through maturity will come through many stages. As with human growth, some Christians get stuck at one stage or another for many years. After birth comes infancy where there is a need to take in the faith. The pastor who finds him or herself involved in caring for a great many very young Christians will find, like the mother of young children, that the work is extremely demanding (1 Thessalonians 2:11).

After infancy and childhood where there is a strong relationship of love and trust between pastor and Christian there often comes a spiritual adolescence where all of the spiritual 'parents' ' values are taken apart and questioned. This, too, can be an alarming and difficult process unless we recognize what is happening. God's desire is for each of us to come to our own mature and adult faith. That process must involve questioning and discussion at each stage of our lives. And just as with adult growth to maturity, the process never comes to an end. Life continually presents new challenges which keep us growing and changing throughout.

Once more we see that role of the pastor is far more than that of teacher. To be an effective spiritual parent involves a genuine relationship of love with those who are being nurtured. This cannot be a dispassionate, 'professional' relationship like a relationship between counsellor and client, doctor and patient, teacher and pupil. As St Paul did, we will need to hold God's people in our hearts and yearn for them with the love of Christ Jesus if we are to see them grow. Yet the pastor's love needs to be of the kind which enables people to develop and does not smother them. Our own children do not grow to maturity through the parents doing everything for them and treating them like babies. They grow through being encouraged to step out and grow away from home and take on an increasing degree of responsibility. They grow not through avoiding the pains of life but through reflecting on those experiences of suffering and of being loved through them. If pastors treat their congregations like children, that is the way they will remain. God's call is to grow to maturity.

Three key stages for the church

The four great pictures of Christian growth in the Scriptures reveal to us that the whole business of building mature Christians is a complex process. Growing to maturity never comes to an end. Within each picture of growth it is possible to describe three key stages.

The first key stage is the immediate nurture, teaching and aftercare received when a person first becomes a Christian. The foundations of the building are being laid at that time. It is this initial period of nurture which was the focus of *Growing New Christians*. The most effective place for that nurture to happen is within the kind of evangelism-nurture group described there.

However, there is a second stage to growth in each picture which demands particular care and attention: the first part of the journey as a Christian; the period when the seed is growing to a first fruitfulness; the time when the basic structure of the building is going up; the era of spiritual childhood and adolescence. It is that period, which normally lasts several years, which is the focus of this book. For the rest of our lives we shall be growing and learning as Christians and we shall need teaching and pastoral care. However, there is a particular need to grow to stability and maturity in the first few years in a number of different areas. New Christians need help in each area. Often they do not receive it and the results are that the churches which do become effective in evangelism remain full of spiritual children and growth is paralysed. It is at this stage where many people get stuck and many churches need practical help. As our own church has grown, our attention has needed to move away from thinking about how to help people become Christians and gain a good foundation to thinking about how to help them come to maturity.

The third key stage lasts not just for a few years but for the rest of our lives. For the whole of our Christian lives we are growing towards maturity – but that growth will be of a different kind after the first few years. Instead of the intensive work of growing and building which is there in the first few years, growth in Key Stage 3 is continual and steadier. A different kind of teaching and pastoral care is needed which concentrates on enabling us to live out our lives and serve our Lord within the world and in the church.[11]

The key stages can be summarized in the table opposite.

It is a lack of understanding of Key Stage 2 which hinders the growth of many churches. We simply expect new Christians to grow up faster than they do. Many are expected to make the leap from Stage 1, where a nurture group is provided, to Stage 3, where there is little special teaching or care, within the first year of becoming a Christian. For many, the gap is simply too wide and people fall away from faith as a result. The whole process of initiation needs to be deeper and last longer. As we shall see from the next chapters, it is a process which involves not only special groups and courses but the life of the whole Christian community.

	Key Stage 1 *Six months*	**Key Stage 2** *Three years*	**Key Stage 3** *The rest of your life*
The journey	Setting out	Being equipped for the journey	Being a pilgrim
Agriculture	Sowing and germination	Bringing to fruitfulness	Seasonal growth and pruning
Building	Laying the foundations	Building the superstructure	Extension, decoration, refurbishment and rebuilding
Parenting	Birth and infancy	Spiritual childhood and adolescence	Growth as an adult

----

Study Guide

TRACK ONE

For Ministers and Church Leaders

Questions for reflection and discussion

1 Try and write your own definition of Christian maturity in two or three sentences. Compare definitions within a wider group.
2 List what is available in your own church situation to help Christians grow in each of the Key Stages 1–3. Where is the biggest gap? What do you need to change?

Ideas for sermons and training courses

1 A sermon series on the four pictures of growth.
2 An all-age worship series on themes and stories from Bunyan's *The Pilgrim's Progress* – possibly over a summer holiday period.

For further reading

How Faith Grows, Jeff Astley and others, National Society/ Church House Publishing, 1991.

<hr/>

TRACK TWO

For Group Leaders

Track Two assumes that each chapter forms the material for one session with your group of about ninety minutes. You may want to take more sessions over some chapters or combine some. It is more important to go at the pace of the group than to fit into a neat syllabus. The material assumes you are working with a group of people who know each other a little bit. The aim behind the exercises is to help the group members experience truth as well as understand it.

Track Two can be used in conjunction with Track Four, which gives daily Bible readings and individual exercises.

<hr/>

KEY STAGES OF CHRISTIAN GROWTH

<hr/>

Introductory exercise

Describe your Christian life so far to a partner by drawing a map of a journey. Mark on it any significant periods of growth; or encounters with God. Indicate any 'ups' or 'downs' or wrong turnings. Where do you think your journey will take you into the future?

If you were advising someone who was just setting out on the Christian life – what equipment would you advise them to take for the journey?

Share your answers briefly with the whole group.

Four pictures of the way we grow

Teaching input from the chapter – possibly illustrated with visuals.

Bible study: the parable of the sower *Luke 8:1–15*

Read through the passage together or in small groups. Identify the different soils, and the obstacles to growth.[12]

One measure of maturity is bearing fruit. What kind of fruit?

Three key stages

Teaching input from the chapter. Illustrate with table of key stages. Ask the group to discuss which key stage they find themselves in.

Prayer exercise

Imagine your life as a temple being built by God for his glory. Are the foundations properly laid? How much of the walls and roof are complete? What materials have been used in the construction? Where is repair and renovation needed? What part of the temple is God working on at present? Do you have a vision of the finished picture?

TRACK THREE

For Those Working One-to-One

For help and guidance in working one-to-one and using this section please see Chapter 3.

Bible study

Read together the parable of the two sons (Luke 15.11–32). Talk about the different stages of the journey.[13] What stage do you feel you are in at the moment?

Key stages of Christian growth

The need to grow as Christians. The four pictures the Bible gives. Three key stages of growth. What is needed now?

Planning for future meetings

The kind of one-to-one help that will be useful in Key Stage 2.

Prayer together

For Those Working on Their Own

Daily Bible readings

Try to listen to God through the daily readings as well as trying to understand them with your mind. You may find it helpful to make a note of the passages you read and anything which strikes you – or any questions which are raised.

Mon: *Luke 15:11–32* The parable of the two sons
Tue: *Luke 8:1–15* The parable of the sower
Wed: *John 15:1–16* The vine and the branches
Thurs: *Galatians 5:16–25* Spiritual fruit
Fri: *Luke 6:47–49; 14:28–30* The builders' parables
Sat: *1 Corinthians 3:1–9* Paul on nurture (1)
Sun: *1 Corinthians 3:10–17* Paul on nurture (2)

Longer exercise

To get the most out of the longer exercises you will need about half an hour's peace and quiet to pray, a Bible, and a notebook and pen to jot down any reflections.

Look back with God over your Christian life until the present time. Thank him for all the good things, all the lessons learned and all the people who have helped you to grow. Take time over this.

If you can, identify times in your own life when growth has seemed like a journey, or a seed coming to maturity or a building under construction.

Commit to God this new stage of your walk with him. Ask him to show you particular areas of your life where you need to build with him. Make a note of them and ask for his help.

Use Psalm 131:1–2 as a prayer of trust in God for the next part of the growing process. Repeat the Psalm several times in your mind as you pray. If you can, learn it by heart and take it into the coming week.

NOTES

1 Isaiah 5:1–7; Psalm 80:8–9; Jeremiah 2:21
2 Matthew 13:1–23; 24–30; Mark 4:26–34
3 John 15
4 1 Corinthians 3:5–9; Galatians 5:16–26
5 Exodus 26–31; 1 Kings 5–8; Amos 7:7–9; Isaiah 61:4
6 Matthew 7:24–27; Luke 14:28–29
7 1 Corinthians 3:16; 6:19 etc
8 Hosea 11:1
9 1 Corinthians 4:15; Galatians 4:19
10 1 Corinthians 3:1; 14:20; Hebrews 5:12; 6:1–3; 1 Peter 2:2
11 Within Key Stage 3 it may be possible to identify a number of different stages of adult faith development. One attempt to do this is provided by James Fowler. In Fowler's observations of adult faith, 'Choosing faith' (his Stage 4) develops into 'Balanced faith' (his Stage 5) and, sometimes, into 'Selfless faith' (his Stage 6). For an introduction to Fowler's work see *How Faith Grows* by Jeff Astley and others, National Society/Church House Publishing, 1991.
12 See *Growing New Christians*, pp. 190–3 for an expositon of the parable as it relates to new Christians.
13 See *Growing New Christians*, pp. 18–24.

two

What is Christian Maturity?

Mike has been a Christian for several years. He's fully involved in the life of the church in terms of worship and ministry. But he feels his knowledge of the faith has hardly grown at all since he first became a Christian. 'It's as though the outline of the jigsaw was filled in several years ago – but I'm still waiting for the middle.' Jane, too, has been a Christian for some time and is active in ministry. She's a good reader and has learned a great deal about the faith – but has real trouble with personal morality. Peter is regularly in church on Sundays and is always there at prayer meetings. He has a genuine concern for evangelism. But if you ask him to sweep the church and wash up after coffee on Sundays you will receive a polite but very firm refusal. Fay has an excellent grasp of what the Christian faith is about; she prays faithfully each night and reads her Bible regularly; but she attends church only on the rare occasion.

All of these people are on the road to Christian maturity. To help them further we need a clear understanding of what our goals are, what Christian maturity is and how we grow towards it.

Maturity is . . . becoming like Jesus

The measure of maturity for a Christian is the character of Jesus Christ. Our goal is to be just like him in every way. It is as we stand next to Jesus that we realize how far we still have to travel and how much building the Lord still has to do in our own lives.

For this reason, the most important books of the Bible

for new Christians to become familiar with are the gospels, especially in Key Stage 2. As new Christians encounter Christ himself in the gospels they will learn about his character and his ways and receive a clear pattern for growth.

Is there any way we can succinctly describe the character of Jesus and the Christian character and maturity we are aiming for? At the beginning of the Sermon on the Mount, Matthew's Gospel presents the heart of Jesus' teaching about character in eight Beatitudes.[1] The sayings not only describe eight threads of Christian maturity but also give a portrait of Jesus himself. They are promises of blessing. Each has many layers of meaning. The words Jesus uses have a long history within the Old Testament and Judaism which would be known to the original readers of Matthew's gospel. There is no better description of the maturity we are aiming for than the Beatitudes. Some understanding of each of the sayings is essential as we reflect on our own aims of presenting ourselves perfect in Christ.

Blessed are the poor in spirit, for theirs is the kingdom of heaven

The first Beatitude contains the whole Gospel. At the heart of our character, if we are mature, we need to recognize that we are spiritually poor. However far we have travelled, we know we have so much further to go. It is only as we recognize our need for God and his grace at each point in our lives that we are able to receive from him. As we come to him with empty hands he is able to fill them. If we come with our hands full of our own achievements then God can give nothing to us.

The Pharisee and the tax collector in the parable Jesus tells illustrate what it means to be spiritually poor.[2] The Pharisee crashes into God's presence as though he has a right to be there and to be acknowledged because of all his goodness. He is so full of himself that his only need for God is to be admired (or worshipped) by his creator. The tax collector is poor in spirit. He stands a long way away, refuses to lift up his face and cries in brokenness of spirit: 'God, have mercy on me a sinner'.

The Laodicean Christians described in Revelation badly need to grow to maturity in Christ. Yet they are prevented from any growth at all by their firm conviction: 'I am rich; I have acquired wealth and do not need a thing'.[3] The risen Christ's call to them is to return to the attitude of spiritual poverty so that growth can begin again.

One of the real dangers of any book or course which aims to teach Christians what it means to be mature is that it will produce pride and a feeling that 'now I have arrived'. It's this very attitude which still infects so many adults who are confirmed and feel that confirmation marks some kind of graduation ceremony. The real test of any teaching on Christian growth and maturity is not only that it should move people further along the road, but that it should give them also a deeper insight into how far they still have to travel. It is that attitude of being poor in spirit which leads to God's people possessing the kingdom of heaven.

Blessed are those who mourn, for they shall be comforted

For many years the second Beatitude puzzled me. What was it doing here in second place in the list? All the other marks of character described here (except possibly the last) could be said to apply to any Christian at any time. So why do we have a word for the bereaved inserted in this particular set of sayings?

The key lies in understanding the word 'mourn'. The second Beatitude is a tremendous word of comfort for the bereaved but it is not primarily addressed to them. All God's people are called to mourn for the suffering of the world, for the state of the Church and for their own sinful lives. We are to weep as Jesus wept over Jerusalem; as the prophets of the Old Testament cry with compassion for the sake of God's people.[4] To mourn is part of Christian maturity.

For the new (or not so new) Christian this involves several things. It means discovering that Christian joy is not a shallow and superficial thing based upon closing our ears to suffering and ignoring pain. It means – in British culture – jettisoning some of what passes for a sense of humour based on sarcasm and ridicule and becoming a serious people in our speech and attitudes. It means acknowledging that the Christian life will involve suffering and pain and grief as well as times of triumph and exaltation – and learning to draw on the resources of faith in those times as much as in the times of joy. In the Book of Psalms there are as many laments as songs of joy. Our modern liturgies and songs do not have the same balance. The Book of Hebrews is written to a community of Christians learning to live out their faith amid great suffering and persecution. The writers are teaching us to be detached from this world and to remember that we are aliens and strangers here; in this world we are continually longing for the world which is to come and in that sense in mourning.

Blessed are the meek, for they will inherit the earth

Meekness is one of the hardest attitudes to define or to understand. It is not weakness – which gives in to anything and everything. Moses is the only individual in the Old Testament described as meek[5] and he is an immensely strong leader. Jesus himself, the servant of God, is described in the Old Testament and the New as meek and gentle,[6] yet he, too, is a strong and forthright person.

Meekness is the opposite in every way of pride and as such is one of the vital characteristics of Christian maturity. A mature Christian is not one who exalts himself or pushes herself forward in any way. A mature Christian will have the grace of meekness and gentleness in every situation, as Jesus does, and in that character will find great blessing and peace. So much striving is taken out of human life if we give up ambition, pride and competition and are content to be the people God has made us.

Jesus demonstrates meekness not only in his character and teaching but in his actions – particularly in his washing of the feet of the disciples.[7] It is that servant heart and action which a Christian growing to maturity will display not only in ministry (things done for God), but in the workplace, home and leisure pursuits.

Blessed are those who hunger and thirst for righteousness, for they will be filled

All the Beatitudes have several layers of meaning. This one is the most obvious. Righteousness at one level means: 'those who long to be right with God'. In Jesus, through his death on the cross, we are counted righteous before God and our sins are forgiven. That longing for righteousness takes shape in us before we become Christians. As we come to Christ that longing is satisfied. Christian maturity is built on the foundation that we are saved by grace through faith. We cannot win God's favour or pay for our own sin. A surprising number of people who have been part of the Church for some time need to hear that basic truth simply and lovingly communicated.

Yet in all growing Christians a hunger and thirst for righteousness will continue beyond conversion into a desire to be holy, an impatience with sin in our lives and a longing to go on growing more like Jesus. The Beatitude's promise is that this longing will be satisfied – partly in this life as God continues to transform us from within (yet never so much as to take that hunger and thirst away) and fully in the life to come when we shall be made perfect in Christ.

Last and not least, there is a third dimension, for our longing is not only to be accounted righteous ourselves, but to see right prevail throughout the world. This is what we mean as we pray each day: 'Your kingdom come; your will be done on earth as in heaven'. Growing to maturity means growing in our awareness of oppression and injustice in the local, national and international communities and coming to play our part in bringing that righteousness about.

Blessed are the merciful, for they will be shown mercy

Religious people can be among the most judgemental people in the world – especially those who consider themselves to be mature and to have arrived; and especially those religious people who have a real concern for holiness. One of the eight key characteristics Jesus outlines in his portrait of maturity is the opposite of judgement: mercy. The more we grow in our Christian faith the more mercy is to be part of our lives and character.

The parable of the beam and the mote is told later in the Sermon on the Mount to address this very point.[8] All of us have a courtroom in our minds. Day by day we continue to bring others to trial in this courtroom for their dress, their manners, their colour, the behaviour of their children, their morals and so on. As we judge others harshly, so we reveal that we ourselves are still some way away from the kingdom.

Our lives, character and conversation are to be shaped and informed by mercy, the steadfast love which is at the heart of God's character. Part of becoming merciful is learning to forgive as we have been forgiven. Again this is a truth which is turned into a prayer by Jesus to be said each day by his disciples: forgive us our sins as we forgive those who sin against us. The mature Christian is not the one who is able to point out the faults of others. The mature Christian is the one who is able to deal with wrongs and hurts in the past and the present, to forgive seventy times seven times and still be ready to forgive some more.

Blessed are the pure in heart, for they will see God

Purity of heart carries a twofold meaning. Holiness is one: a desire for our will and attitudes and emotions – the centre of our being – to be made clean. The working out of our baptism and cleansing by Christ takes a lifetime. In the initial years of being a Christian it is the larger, most obvious areas of sin which God will deal with first. The longer we walk with him, the deeper his light will shine into our lives.

To be pure in heart also means to be single-minded in our motives and love of God. Growing in maturity means that we come more and more to fulfil the first commandment in Jesus' summary of the law: 'Love the Lord your God with all your heart and with all your soul and with all your strength and with all your mind'. In the Old Testament the Lord's complaint about his people is that they are not single-minded in their devotion to him and often turn away to other gods, committing spiritual adultery. The kind of love God seeks in us is that single-minded and faithful love a man should have for his wife and a woman for her husband. As we grow in the Christian life we should be growing in purity of heart. Jesus himself has such a powerful love for the Father and for the Father's will that it can sustain him through both Gethsemane and Calvary.

And to be pure in heart means to be able to see God. We see the Lord as in a reflection in the dirty mirror of our own hearts and lives.[9] As we become, little by little, pure in heart, so our picture of God becomes clearer and clearer: less a reflection of ourselves and more a true likeness.

Blessed are the peacemakers, for they will be called sons of God

Jesus Christ, the Son of God, is a peacemaker. His whole life was dedicated to reconciling man to God and men and women to each other. That work of peacemaking and reconciliation involved laying down his own life in every way and eventually led to the cross.[10]

The seventh mark of Christian maturity is growing into a peacemaker in every area of life: seeking peace within families, in the workplace and in every environment we enter. We are called to engage also in the central act of making peace: joining in Christ's work of reconciling men and women to God. To be a peacemaker means to take on gladly the work of an evangelist and witness to Christ's work in our lives.

As with Jesus, so in our lives, the work of peacemaking will be costly and involve laying down our own lives in the work of the Gospel and in the cause of reconciliation. We may find ourselves used by God in large or small ways to bring peace but we will soon discover that it is the peacemakers who stand in the angry area between two sides and it is often the peacemakers who are wounded. To grow as a Christian means to take on the calling of reconciliation.

Blessed are those who are persecuted because of righteousness, for theirs is the kingdom of heaven

The final Beatitude is the most radical of all as a measure

of maturity, especially to comfortable Christians in modern Britain. Its meaning is that we have not attained the character of Christ until we provoke a hostile reaction from some of those around us; we are not living the Christian life as it should be lived until we are persecuted for the sake of righteousness.

Abbé Michel Quoist writes in his preface to the prayer 'All': 'The Gospel preached in its utter purity exalts, frightens or shocks. It is bound to meet with violent reactions as it is diametrically opposed to sinful man and "the world". When a man really hears the Gospel, his whole life must be reassessed, if he is sincere, for the demands of Christ do not countenance half measures.'[11]

By this measure, the Church in Britain has a long way still to travel from lay people to bishops. Our lives and our words do not provoke any hostile reaction in those around us. Our lifestyle is often indistinguishable from that of our neighbours with the exception of attending church on Sundays. Jesus had such a quality of holiness about him that those he encountered who did not choose to follow him wanted to drive him from the world. The Church is called to walk the same path. We are not to welcome persecution and difficulty, but we are to regard them as a sign that we are on the right lines and becoming more the Church Christ calls us to be. The Christian faith is not a comfortable add-on for modern Western man and woman to assuage guilt, heal disorder and give security for heaven. Jesus' call to discipleship is to a radical and costly change. A sign of that change will be persecution.

Growth in different dimensions

The Beatitudes give us a picture of Christian growth which is about far more than learning Bible verses or how to be a responsible member of the Church. We are to grow up into the character of Jesus and that growth will take us the rest of our lives.

We often think of Christian growth as a progression along a line, learning a certain set of truths or standards in a definite order. That is an unhelpful picture. The truth is that we are growing in a number of different dimensions at the same time.

Paul writes to the Romans: 'I myself am convinced that you yourselves are full of goodness, complete in knowledge and competent to instruct one another.'[12] Maturity here is not a matter of growing in one direction only (such as knowledge of the faith). It has at least three dimensions: reflecting Christ in the way we live our lives (goodness), understanding our faith and knowing God (knowledge), and the ministry of building up others in the faith (competent to instruct one another). So, unlike the initial journey to faith, growth to Christian maturity cannot be thought of as moving people along a simple line marked by stages. It is much better to think of a person's Christian life growing outwards along a number of different spokes of a wheel like this:

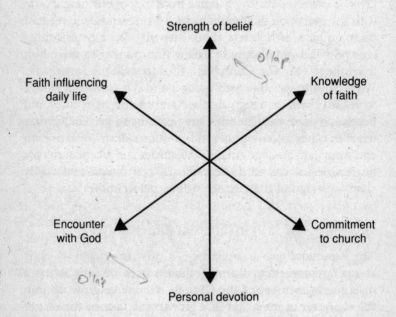

Strength of belief

O'lap

Faith influencing
daily life

Knowledge
of faith

Encounter
with God

Commitment
to church

O'lap

Personal devotion

Weakness — mission, serving not explicit

Strength of belief:[13] how deeply does a person believe? Is faith growing or declining with the years?

Knowledge of faith: is there a learning and a growing in knowledge of the Scriptures and the Christian tradition?

Commitment to the church: is this growing and deepening with the years and being expressed in practical ministry?

Personal devotion: can a person pray and sustain a life of deepening prayer?

Encounter with God: within prayer and worship and the whole of life is there a deepening and growing sense of meeting with and listening to God?

Faith influencing daily life: is Christian faith being earthed in family life, personal ethics, working practices and so on?

This is not meant to be a complete list of the dimensions of Christian growth. Far more spokes would be needed. But it does give a better picture than a straight line of the kind of growing that is involved. A person's growth to maturity should be thought of not as a point on a line but as a different shaped 'blob' on the star drawn by linking together relative strengths or weaknesses on each line. More often than not a person (and a church) will be growing more in some dimensions than in others. A church may have a strong tradition of Bible teaching and so its members may be strong in their knowledge of faith, commitment to church and personal devotion, but very weak in the way faith influences daily life, any sense of encounter with God and any sense of faith growing. An individual may have a very strong faith and a rich series of encounters with God, but be very patchy in his or her commitment to church.

Keeping the star-grid in mind can be a valuable pastoral tool when thinking about growth with individuals or a church. This person needs to grow – but in what dimension is that growth especially needed? Once that question has been answered, it's much easier to begin planning a strategy to enable growth to happen. One person will need equipping with the tools needed to read the Bible for himself. Another will need teaching in the basics of how to pray. Yet another will need help in working out the implications of faith in marriage and family life. Examining the tools for the task of building is the subject of the next chapter.

Study Guide

TRACK ONE

For Ministers and Church Leaders

Questions for reflection and discussion

1 Draw a 'star grid' for the following:
   (a) Your own church
   (b) Two or three individuals within the church with different degrees of maturity
   (c) Yourself

   What conclusions do you draw?
2 Take the Beatitudes as a theme for further reflection and study over the next few months. Read one of the gospels right through and note ways in which Jesus lives out the Beatitudes in his life, ministry and teaching.
3 Using the star-grid, work out some headings for a pastoral conversation with a member of your congregation to review the way in which they are growing in the Christian life.

Ideas for sermons and training courses

A sermon series or parish weekend on the Beatitudes.

For further reading

The Imitation of Christ, Thomas à Kempis, Penguin, 1952.
Winning Them Back, Eddie Gibbs, Monarch, 1993.
Prayers of Life, Michel Quoist, Macmillan, 1963.

TRACK TWO
_____

For Group Leaders

WHAT IS CHRISTIAN MATURITY?
_____

Introductory exercise

Ask each person in the group to write down a short definition of Christian maturity. Pool your answers on a flip chart.

Bible study

Read the Beatitudes together (Matthew 5:3–10). Give a short introduction to the passage and why you are studying it.

Working in twos or threes, ask each person to select two Beatitudes: the one they like best and the one which they find most difficult either to understand or to live up to. Go round the group sharing your findings.

Becoming like Jesus

A short exposition of the Beatitudes using material from the chapter.

Growth in different dimensions

Teaching input from the chapter using a visual of the star-grid. Ask people to reflect in small groups which dimensions they need to grow in most of all. How can the group help them to do that?

Prayer exercise

You may find it helpful to light a candle and place it in the centre of the room and turn out the electric lights.

Ask one member of the group to read out the Beatitudes one by one with silence in between.

After each Beatitutde is read out members of the group lead in prayers of confession and intercession. This can be spontaneous or prepared.

Ask the Lord for grace to grow.

For Those Working One-to-One

What is Christian maturity?

Share your ideas together.

Bible study

Read the Beatitudes together (Matthew 5:3–10). Talk about each quality in turn with illustrations from life or from the gospels.

Growing in different dimensions

Draw and explain the star-grid and each draw a chart for yourselves. Compare where you are now with where you need to grow. This may affect the order in which you tackle sessions 8–12.

Prayer together

For Those Working on Their Own

Daily Bible readings

The readings this week are all descriptions of Jesus from different sections of the Bible:

Mon: *Isaiah 42:1–9* The servant of the Lord
Tue: *Matthew 11:25–30* Jesus' invitation
Wed: *John 1:1–14* The Word of God
Thurs: *Philippians 2:1–11* The song of Christ's glory
Fri: *Colossians 1:15–23* The surpemacy of Christ
Sat: *Ephesians 1:3–14* Blessings in Christ
Sun: *Revelation 1:9–19* John's vision of Jesus

Longer exercise

Take an audit of your Christian growth using the Beatitudes.

Taking each in turn ask yourself whether this quality is present in your life. Is it evident in you within your family, within your workplace and within your church?

Which two Beatitudes do you need to work on most? Ask God to show you what steps to take.

NOTES

1 Matthew 5:3–10. Verses 11 and 12, which contain a ninth 'Blessed. . .' saying are really an expansion of the eighth Beatitude and the beginning of a new section of the sermon.
2 Luke 18:9–14
3 Revelation 3:17
4 Jeremiah 9:1
5 Numbers 12:3 – 'Now Moses was a very humble man, more humble than anyone on the face of the earth.' The word translated 'humble' by the NIV occurs only here in the Old Testament applied to an individual.
6 Isaiah 42:1–4; Zechariah 9:9;1 Corinthians 10:1; Philippians 2:6–11
7 John 13:1–17
8 Matthew 7:1–5
9 1 Corinthians 13:12
10 Colossians 1:20
11 Michel Quoist, *Prayers of Life*, Macmillan, 1963, p. 82.
12 Romans 15:14
13 This list of six dimensions of growth is adapted from Eddie Gibbs, *Winning Them Back*, Monarch, 1993, pp. 22ff. Eddie Gibbs is himself using categories developed by religious sociologists, Stark and Glock. The advantage of these categories is that they are to some degree objective and measurable.

three

The Tools for the Task

I have a friend who is a carpenter. If he were to turn up one day to do a job without his tools he would not make much impact on site. We can't saw wood with our hands or drill holes with our fingers or hammer in nails with our feet. We need hammers, saws, plumb lines and a workbench to make a building.

The same is true for those of us called to the ministry of building mature Christians – and if I understand the New Testament correctly that means every one of us. We need a clear understanding of what Christian maturity is – the plans. But we cannot then start work with our bare hands. We need the right tools for the job of helping people to grow. It probably takes less time to learn to use these tools than it takes to learn how to use a lathe or a saw correctly. Yet surprisingly few Christians are prepared to invest that time and so we remain ineffective in the building work. There are five tools we need to come to grips with.

Tool one: prayer

Christian growth is God's work from beginning to end. For that reason prayer is essential. I find that encouraging and challenging at the same time. It is encouraging because you don't need a lot of knowledge or education to help people grow to maturity as Christians. You don't even need to be in the same place or meeting with them regularly. But we do need faith and a vision to intercede for new Christians and we do need some understanding of how to pray.

For this understanding we turn to St Paul. Paul spent most

of his ministry building mature Christians. His letters are written to new churches giving them advice and encouragement in the first few years of their Christian faith. Paul is the master builder in this whole ministry of Christian growth.[1] It is clear as we read the Epistles that the foundation of his ministry was to pray for those who were growing in Christ.

On some occasions that prayer was a work of joy.[2] The news from a particular church or individual was good. There was real cause to thank God. Praying for people in those circumstances was not difficult. On other occasions prayer was much more like a wrestling match. Paul writes to the Christians in Colossae: 'I want you to know how much I am struggling for you and for those at Laodicea and for all those who have not met me personally.'[3] The Greek word 'struggle' is 'agona' – the word from which we get 'agony'. Later in the same letter Paul uses the word to describe the experience of his friend Epaphras in his prayer for the same people: 'He is always wrestling in prayer for you that you may stand firm in the will of God. . .'[4] Paul uses even stronger language to describe his prayers for the Christians in Galatia, who are facing a complete crisis in their faith: 'My dear children, for whom I am again in the pains of childbirth until Christ is formed in you, how I wish I could be with you now and change my tone because I am perplexed about you.'[5]

For Paul, intercession is not a perfunctory act performed out of guilt or duty. This is a vital labour of love essential to the building of the kingdom of God in people's lives. That building is spiritual work and must be done primarily by spiritual means. Many of us in the Church at the present time who are called to care for and build up the faith of new Christians have much to learn. My guess is that most pastors (whether lay or ordained) give very little time or energy to intercessory prayer. When we do intercede our intercessions consist simply of reading through a list of names and lifting them before God. If we set our practice beside St Paul's, we have much to learn not only from his passion for prayer but from what he prayed.

Paul is very specific in his prayers. He almost always has

grounds for thanksgiving which precede intercession. The prayer which follows is asking for particular grace for particular churches. It is as though Paul can see, through the grace of the Holy Spirit, a picture of the church as it now is, and therefore knows exactly where to direct his prayer. He has learned to join his intercession with that of the Spirit who searches the hearts and minds of men. Prayer can then grow from being a vague petition to God to bless Fred or Jane to being a precise tool in the building process; thanking God for areas of strength in a new Christian's life and praying specifically for areas of weakness. The evidence from Paul's ministry is that God blesses and answers that very specific way of praying and new Christians are enabled to grow up into Christ.

Praying for individuals in this way is very time-consuming and needs energy. We need more than a snatched five minutes at the beginning or end of the day for our prayers. No doubt some will be called to intercede as a specific ministry in a special way. But all of us concerned to build Christian maturity in others need to begin by developing our own life of prayer.

Tool two: example

George Herbert was a country vicar and a preacher as well as a poet. This is one of his poems, 'The Windows', about the relationship between what we say and who we are. If you are not used to Herbert's poetry you may need to read it several times.

> Lord, how can man preach thy eternal word?
>   He is a brittle, crazy glass;
> Yet in thy temple thou dost him afford
>   This glorious and transcendent place
>   To be a window, through thy grace.
>
> But when thou dost anneal in glass thy story,
>   Making thy life to shine within
> The holy Preachers, then the light and glory
>   More rev'rend grows and more doth win;
>   Which else shows waterish, bleak and thin.

> Doctrine and life, colours and life in one
>   When they combine and mingle, bring
> A strong regard and awe; but speech alone
>   Doth vanish like a flaring thing,
>   And in the ear, not conscience, ring.

The God we proclaim is a God who believes in teaching by example. He does not merely tell us that he loves us. He shows his love in the gift of his Son. He does not simply teach us what it means to be holy. He demonstrates that holiness through the Word of God who was made flesh and lives among us. In the same way Jesus demonstrated the kingdom of God by the person he was as well as teaching his followers through words. The parables show us that the smallest of our actions speak volumes about our hearts: how we give our offering, where we say our prayers, where we sit at table when invited to a feast and how we deal with noisy little children who intrude on our peace. Jesus not only teaches his disciples to be a servant; he washes their feet.

Exactly the same challenge is presented to anyone called to the ministry of building up others in faith. Our actions and the people we are will speak far more powerfully than our words. Little children learn how to talk, to crawl and to do most things by imitating others. They don't learn by attending a six-week course on standing upright. They look around, see everyone else moving around on their two feet and begin to try to stand. Whether we like it or not (and most of us do not) we, too, are called to be examples.

When Paul encourages new Christians to imitate him he is consciously using his example as a tool in the work of building others in Christian maturity.[6] Timothy and Titus are both encouraged by Paul to 'set an example for the believers in speech, in life, in love, in faith and in purity'.[7] The writers to the Hebrews advise the believers there to grow by imitating the faith of the leaders who first brought them to Christ.[8] Part of the ministry of building mature Christians is building with the example of our own lives. 'Whatever you have learned or received or heard from me, *or seen in me* – put into practice. And the God of peace will be with you.'

Building mature Christians means far more than preaching sermons or leading a group or meeting occasionally with a younger Christian for mutual help and encouragement. The primary way we build maturity and discipleship is by example. The challenge of being an example to others needs to affect our whole lives. How can we teach others to pray if our own relationship with God is dry and empty? How can we encourage others in disciplines of worship if we ourselves are not in church regularly? How can we help others to be self-controlled in speech and keep confidences if we so obviously enjoy a good gossip?

Does this mean that those called to this ministry need to believe we have reached the stage of perfection? This is not Paul's view – nor should it be ours. We have already seen that Christian maturity is not a destination that we travel towards and then reach. It is much more a series of attitudes. One of the most important for those building others in faith is described in Philippians 3. Paul takes some time to set out his own personal goals in life and in maturity (vv. 7–11): to gain Christ and be found in him, to know the power of his resurrection and the fellowship of his sufferings and to attain the resurrection from the dead. This is the destination. But Paul then goes to great lengths to explain that he does not believe he has arrived. For him, maturity lies in 'forgetting what is behind and straining towards what is ahead'. It is the attitude of the traveller not the point he has reached which is more central.

Those who set the best examples to new Christians will be those who realize that they have most to learn themselves about every aspect of the Christian life. These people's lives will say to those learning from them: 'I haven't arrived yet. I know the example I set may be very flawed. But if you can, learn from me.' People who think in this way will always succeed in pointing beyond themselves to Jesus.

The worst teachers will be those who believe they have arrived and say through their words or in their lives: 'I'm a mature Christian now (especially now I can wear a dog collar). Look at how wise and good I am. I have so much to teach you. Learn from me.' Teachers with this attitude are too full of their own perfection. They may find some disciples to build up their own following but hardly ever succeed in pointing people to Jesus.

The greatest example we need to set is in being continual learners and travellers ourselves. That will mean being constantly willing to be changed by God, allowing him to put his finger on this or that area of our lives and being willing to work with him, over time, to transform us. If we are going to help and minister to others, we shall need to be willing to accept that help and ministry ourselves. The calling to build Christians to maturity engages with the whole of our lives.

Tool three: the word of God

Paul's second letter to Timothy is an excellent handbook for a minister charged with bringing young churches to maturity. Paul writes there, in two places, of using the word of God as a tool in the process of building Christians:

> Do your best to present yourself to God as one approved, a workman who does not need to be ashamed and who correctly handles the word of truth (2:15)

> All Scripture is God-breathed and is useful for teaching, rebuking, correcting and training in righteousness so that the man of God may be thoroughly equipped for every good work (3:16, 17)

One of the main tools God has given us for the building work is the living and active word of God. Anyone concerned to be a builder needs to become familiar with the Scriptures in the first place and, second, to learn how to use them. Familiarity with the Bible can only come from reading Scripture and hearing it read and applied over a number of years. Not all of us have been taught the Holy Scriptures from infancy, as Timothy had. But all of us engaged in building work need a strong discipline of personal Bible reading and study to feed and to supplement all of the teaching which is taking place.

The ways in which the Scriptures are used in the building

of maturity will vary from person to person and from church to church. There is a particular need for good biblical preaching in any church where people are going to grow to maturity. It is a wise man who has said that 'sermonettes make Christianettes'.[9] Godly preaching is a dynamic activity in which the living God encounters the minds and hearts and lives of the congregation through his written and living word. That means that time needs to be given to preaching both in terms of preparation and in terms of the time allocated to the sermon within Sunday services.

To bring a congregation to maturity a wider range of texts will need to be addressed than the one provided in the ASB lectionary for Holy Communion. Particular books of the Bible will need to be explored through expository series of sermons. Specific themes and doctrines can be addressed in one-off sermons or in a short series. Care also needs to be taken to address the actual issues people require help with rather than the ones we imagine they need to hear about. For this to happen good feedback on the preaching from the congregation is essential. Questionnaires asking for suggestions for future sermons or sermon series can be useful.[10] Throughout this book ideas for sermons and sermon series are suggested in the practical section at the end of each chapter. Help is available in a number of other publications mentioned in the study guide.

Preaching which builds maturity has a prophetic edge. That is, it is not just concerned to address wider social and political issues through the Scriptures, but the themes of the preaching arise directly from the preacher listening to God about where the congregation are and what they need to hear.

On occasions that listening to God will happen through what people are saying. During one of our regular visiting missions earlier this year the team taking part were very disappointed at the lack of support for the mission from the wider church both in terms of visitors and those coming to pray. It became clear through subsequent discussions that, as a church, we had lost our zeal and enthusiasm for the work of evangelism and our sense of its importance. We needed to address that situation primarily through preaching. That happened not in the next fortnight but about two months later at the start of a new term with a short series of three sermons on evangelism at each service.

At other times, that listening to God will come through meditation on his word and through prayer by the preacher. Several years ago we passed through a time of real change in the life of the church as we divided our morning service into two to make room for more people. This step itself was taken in response to a number of prophetic words we had been given which had been properly weighed and owned by the congregation. Two months into the change I had an overwhelming sense that something was wrong in the church but I couldn't put my finger on exactly what. This troubled feeling continued to grow until one evening the Lord said to me, through a quiet inner voice that I have learned to recognize as his, 'The church has caught a moaning disease. You need to rebuke it.' At once the nature of the problem fell into place. Like the Israelites in the wilderness, people were not liking the place to which God had led us. The sermon I preached the following Sunday evening was one of the most uncomfortable and direct I have delivered. No doubt it was also hard to listen to. The message was very simple: 'God says we have caught a moaning disease like the Israelites. Either the moaning stops or the blessing stops. It's up to you.' God's word is powerful, however inadequately delivered. Once the problem had been identified and its spiritual roots exposed and challenged, people were able to respond, correct their behaviour and continue to grow.

Preaching is not, of course, the only way in which the Scriptures are used as a tool for building maturity. There are a variety of environments in church life which give an opportunity for teaching from the Bible. Those with the gift of teaching need to be valued and encouraged by the church. Small groups provide an excellent setting for Bible teaching. In an environment where many of the group members are new Christians a flexible teaching style can work much better than the conventional Bible study where members are simply sharing their ignorance of what the Scriptures teach. Studying and applying the Scriptures one-to-one is also a powerful use of this particular tool of grace. More is said on this below.

In all of this equipping of the saints through Scripture and the teaching ministry there needs to be a balance between the fourfold use of the Bible mentioned in 2 Timothy 3:16. The verse has become important to me in thinking through the issue of discipleship. Paul speaks of using Scripture to teach, rebuke, correct and train. Very often, in our own use of the Bible, we do the first of these but leave out the other three.

One of my children is currently learning to play the trumpet. On those occasions when he remembers to practise strange noises are heard from behind the living room door. If he is ever to master the trumpet, Paul will need to receive all four elements of the learning process mentioned in 2 Timothy 3:16. He will need to be taught about the trumpet and about music and the rudiments of how to play it. This is, as it were, classroom knowledge. He will also need to be corrected from time to time as he plays a wrong note, holds the instrument in the wrong way or interprets the music badly. His teacher would not be doing his job if the mistakes were ignored. There will be a need, on occasion, for rebuke as well as correction: 'You simply haven't practised enough this week, Paul' or 'That was terrible. Come on, you can do better than that.' And finally there will be a need for training: that part of learning which is more than theory; the practical experience passed on from one musician to another about how to get the best out of a musical instrument. Building a competent trumpet player involves all four elements.

Is it not the same with a Christian disciple? Yet as I look at my own ministry I find I am very eager and ready to teach and encourage people in their discipleship and, where I can, to train them. But how often, on the basis of Scripture, am I ready to correct and rebuke when mistakes are made? Learning to do exactly that needs to be a real point of growth for many of us as we learn to build disciples with the tool of Scripture.

Tool four: Christian community

According to Paul, real maturity of faith comes about when the right gifts and ministries are released within the body of the church. It is for this reason, to build mature Christians, that God has given some to be apostles, some to be prophets, some to be evangelists and some to be pastors and teachers.[11] Any work of building should therefore be seen as a team effort not an individual enterprise. For that reason the business of growing to maturity has to be seen in the context of the whole of church life and not as the task of one particular group or course within the church.

It is as we rub up against each other in genuine Christian community that growth will take place. This will be partly through imitation and example as explored above, but partly also through the simple interaction of Christian lives. It is through community that people are encouraged both in their faith and basic disciplines and also in ministry. Friendships grow and basic lessons are learned in giving. Needs and hurts can be shared and care given and received. Visions and dreams can be explored together. Love can begin to grow.

It is in community as well that we learn the harder lessons of our Christian lives. We will not naturally get on with every Christian we meet. Some will annoy and irritate us profoundly. St Benedict, in his rule for enabling Christians to live together, says that these people especially are the means of God's grace to us.[12] Through them we learn to love difficult people. We are spiritually stretched through the experience and we grow. It is the grit in the oyster which is the beginning of the pearl. In the same way it is the person we can't stand who is the greatest challenge to our love and forgiveness and the person God can use most in helping us on. This is what it means to be a church. It's the way God planned it.

But this level of community is only possible if people really do know each other and are prepared to be involved in each others' lives. In order to use the tool of community in building maturity and love we need to be prepared to develop community and fellowship within the church. The precise structures will vary depending on church size and culture. Encouraging the grace of hospitality is a first requirement. Beyond that, most churches have found small groups extremely valuable as a means of establishing and maintaining fellowship in a more meaningful way than through a large congregation.

Growing New Christians explores the role of evangelism-nurture groups in Key Stage 1: laying the foundation for a person's experience of Christ and the church. In Key Stage 2 a different kind of group is needed. Until recently in our own church people transferred directly from a Christians for Life group into the life of an ongoing home group. However, along with a number of other churches around the country, we are now seeking to develop growth groups for Key Stage 2 to follow on from the Christians for Life courses. The growth groups differ from home groups in that they have a more definite teaching content from the leader which will follow a clearly laid out course over a one to two-year period. The syllabus they will follow is approximately the one described in this book. People can, of course, drop out of the group at any time. The growth groups meet a need for more systematic teaching on the part of adults who have become Christians. They also give new Christians a group in which to work through many of the basic issues which come up in the first two to three years of living the Christian life.

Tool five: working one-to-one

Over four hundred years ago the puritan Richard Baxter published *The Reformed Pastor*.[13] The book is a handbook of pastoral care. Its main recommendation is that a clergyman should spend a great deal of his time with individuals and families in his parish. Like Paul we should teach in public places but also from house to house. The purpose of that time should not be polite conversation and passing the time of day, nor even concerned enquiries about the families' health or well-being, but detailed personal instruction about the basics of the Christian faith as outlined in the catechism.

Baxter urges many strong reasons for this individual instruction of families. One memorable section is headed: 'It will help to preserve many ministers from idleness and misspending their time'. He draws attention to the difficulty of the task ('I think it an easier matter by far to compose and preach a good sermon than to deal rightly with an ignorant man for his instruction in the more essential principles of religion') and gives detailed advice on how this individual visiting is to be carried out.

Baxter's work was extremely effective and had a lasting effect on the town of Kidderminster where he lived. The details of his book seem dated now but the principle is surely a good one. If teaching and instruction in church services and in groups is to be effective this must be backed up with a one-to-one ministry. I don't mean by this simple parish visiting which can be valuable in some circumstances and a great waste of time in others. Nor do I mean one-to-one ministry in pastoral counselling, sorting out problems and difficulties as they arise – which is obviously important. What is meant is systematic instruction in the faith individually, where questions can be asked and answered and truth applied to the circumstances of daily lives.

Clearly an ordained person in a parish will only be able to give that kind of individual instruction to very few people and it may not be the best use of his or her time. We are currently working on a discipleship scheme in St George's which will involve linking a new Christian with someone more established in the faith of the same sex and of a similar age and social background. Under the scheme the older and newer Christians will meet together once a fortnight for a twelve-month period and work through some Bible studies together based upon the material in the later chapters of this book. The relationship will be partly one of teaching, partly pastoral and partly simple welcome and friendship and will supplement what is already happening through Christians for Life and growth groups. There will be some oversight of what is happening; the arrangement will be entirely voluntary and can be ended at any time by either party. Our hope is that not only will the scheme help those who are new to the faith but that it will also introduce many established Christians to a pastoral and teaching ministry.

The scheme is designed to run for only the first year or two of a person's Christian life and then lead into some form of spiritual direction where the newer Christian will meet less frequently (about every two to three months) with a more experienced partner to think about prayer and general spiritual growth. It is this kind of relationship which is envisaged in the modern Roman Catholic sacrament of reconciliation. The idea of ongoing face to face spiritual guidance is replacing the old form of anonymous confession through a grill in the wall.

Not all churches will be able to (or will need to) offer a systematic scheme like the one outlined above. But somewhere in the total make-up of teaching and pastoral care in the church there will need to be space for one-to-one work not just to sort out problems but to teach and to build. The more people who can be equipped and involved in this ministry in particular the more securely the whole body will grow up into maturity.

At each of the key stages outlined in Chapter 1 a Christian person needs to receive different things from the congregation as a whole, from the small group and from individual help. These are summarized in the table opposite.

It is no easy task to structure the life of the church so that the Gospel is proclaimed to enquirers and those outside, new Christians are well taught and mature believers are stretched and encouraged in their faith. Learning to use the tools God has given us for the task is a first step.

	Key Stage 1 *Six months*	**Key Stage 2** *Three years*	**Key Stage 3** *The rest of your life*
Congregation	Welcome and initial friendships. Accessible worship. Evangelistic preaching.	Incorporation into the family. Space and encouragement to exercise a ministry. Nourishing worship. Good basic teaching and preaching.	Giving and receiving love in the family. Growth in ministry. Worship which feeds and sustains a mature Christian. Preaching which teaches and stretches.
Small group	*Evangelism–nurture group* Learning the facts. Laying the foundations. Establishing friendships.	*Discipleship/ growth group* More sustained teaching. Learning and growing together.	*Fellowship/ ministry group* Teaching each other from Scripture. Fellowship and support.
One to one	Evangelism. Initial support.	Counselling and inner healing. Teaching and discipling.	Spiritual direction. General pastoral oversight.

Study Guide

TRACK ONE

For Ministers and Church Leaders

Questions for reflection and discussion

1 Take an afternoon off and carry out an audit of your own prayer life with particular emphasis on intercession. What is the next step in developing this vital tool for building?

2 Review what is happening in your own church for Christians in Key Stages 1, 2 and 3 using the table as a guide.
List the things which are already done well.
Is there anything missing completely?
Which section needs the most immediate attention?
Construct an action plan for that area of the church's life.

Ideas for sermons and training courses

1 A sermon or sermon series on intercessory prayer, taking Paul as a guide.

2 A sermon series or group leaders training programme on the five tools for building maturity.

3 A training course on working one to one to set up a discipleship scheme.[14]

4 Develop the idea of spiritual direction for those who have been Christians for several years. What practical steps do you need to take?

For further reading

For those wanting to go deeper into different models of pastoral care down the centuries, Richard Baxter and George Herbert are both well worth reading.

For those wanting to develop intercession and other spiritual disciplines, Richard Foster's book, *Celebration of Discipline*, Hodder and Stoughton, 1980, is an excellent starter.

For Group Leaders

THE TOOLS FOR THE TASK

Introductory exercise

Share in small groups. What helps you to grow as a Christian? Make a list of different things and then number them in order of priority. Share your answers with the whole group.

Helping one another

Teaching input from the chapter – illustrated with visuals and Bible passages – on prayer, example and using Scripture.

Bible study: the body of Christ *1 Corinthians 12:12–30*

Read through the passage together in small groups.
What is Paul saying about our relationship to each other?
How then should we treat each other?

Prayer exercise

Intercession for one another. Divide into small groups of three or four. Each member of the group should share briefly how they need to grow. Pray for each other like Epaphras prayed (Colossians 4:12).

  Make a commitment to go on praying for each other in that way in the week to come.

For Those Working One-to-One

How do Christians help each other to grow?

Share ideas together, including ideas from the chapter.

Bible study

Read Ephesians 4:1–16. Draw out the teaching in the passage about the Body of Christ and different ministries given to the Body for building people to maturity.

Scripture and community

Talk together about the importance of Scripture and using the Bible to teach, rebuke, correct and train in righteousness. How do you both relate to the church? What is good and useful? Is anything lacking? The importance of commitment to the Christian family.

TRACK FOUR

For Those Working on Their Own

Daily Bible readings

Paul's thanksgiving and prayers for growing Christians; Paul's teaching on the Body of Christ.

Mon: *Colossians 1:3–13* Prayer for Christians in Colossae
Tue: *Philippians 1:3–11* Prayer for Christians in Philippi
Wed: *Ephesians 3:14–21* Prayer for Christians in Ephesus
Thurs: *1 Thessalonians 1:2–10* Prayer for Christians in Thessalonica
Fri: *Ephesians 4:1–16* Christ is the head of the Body
Sat: *1 Corinthians 12:12–30* Many parts, one body
Sun: *Romans 12:1–21* Living as the Body of Christ

Longer exercise

Take some time to think about the way you pray for other people.
Whom should you be praying for?
Write a list of family; friends; people in the church; people in the wider community.
How should you pray?
Choose one of Paul's prayers from the daily readings. Write out your own prayer based on the Bible passage to use in your intercessions in the coming weeks.
Make a commitment to intercede regularly for the people on your list.

NOTES

1 1 Corinthians 3:10
2 Philippians 1:4
3 Colossians 2:1
4 Colossians 4:12–13
5 Galatians 4:19–20
6 1 Corinthians 4:17; Philippians 4:8–9; see also James 3:1
7 Titus 2:6–8; 1 Timothy 4:12
8 Hebrews 13:7
9 A saying credited to Campbell Morgan and Stuart Holden by
   John Stott, *I Believe in Preaching*, Hodder and Stoughton, 1982,
   p. 294.
10 For ideas on this see *Mastering Contemporary Preaching* by Hybels,
   Briscoe and Robinson, IVP, 1991, especially Chapters 3 and
   12.
11 Ephesians 4:11–13
12 *Households of God*, ed. David Parry, OSB, Darton, Longman &
   Todd, 1980.
13 Richard Baxter, *The Reformed Pastor*, first published 1656 and still
   available in paperback from The Banner of Truth Trust.
14 Ideas and handouts for this are available from St George's
   House, Lee Mount, Halifax, HX3 5BT.

four

Understanding the Opposition

Mandy was a Christian for six months before she lost interest and fell away from faith – the excuse was that someone at church had offended her. Jane couldn't make the choice between what her boyfriend was asking of her and her fledgling Christianity. Harry found that the demands of his business gradually drew him away from active membership of the church. Jim gave in to the continual pressure from his friends and the soccer club and the teasing from his parents. Ernest succumbed to a persistent temptation and simply felt a failure so he gradually stopped coming to church. The list goes on.

Many of the people I have known who have made a good start in their Christian lives have sooner or later drifted away or stopped growing. Sometimes that has been because I have not cared for them properly or prayed for them enough or because they have been hurt or neglected by others in the church. But often it has been because, for different reasons, they themselves have not persevered in the journey and come to a point of maturity.

The picture given all the way through the Bible is that it is actually very difficult to follow God's ways wholeheartedly. Many do give up and turn back to an easier life. Throughout the history of Israel, from the Exodus to the Exile and beyond, it was only a minority of the people who were faithful to God's call and his ways. In the gospels many people begin to follow Jesus and listen to his teaching but turn back when the teaching becomes difficult and the way demanding. Jesus himself describes the way that leads to salvation as narrow and difficult 'and only a few find it'.[1] In the parable of the sower, told to encourage his disciples, he emphasizes that many people will start out on their Christian lives and, for different reasons, not come to maturity. The same warning is sounded again and again in the New Testament letters and Revelation. Not everyone who sets out will complete the journey.

That is because, to stay with the journey picture, we are travelling through hostile territory. Like Christian on his travels in *The Pilgrim's Progress*, we face many dangers and much opposition as we seek to follow Christ and grow to maturity. It is not simply a matter of sticking to a certain set of rules or making a series of steps in the right order. There is opposition to be faced and a battle to be fought, which is the subject of this chapter.

Those who are caring for new Christians and helping others to grow will find their ministry, in most situations, an extremely demanding one. Sometimes, despite all our teaching and prayer and encouragement, people seem to make such little progress in their Christian lives or else they take a wrong turning which leads them off-course altogether or even just drift away. Those called to this ministry need to understand the dynamic of battle as well. Despite all the help we may be giving, there are strong forces working against the process of Christian growth as well as for it. It is only natural to be disappointed when someone stops moving forward in their Christian life or comes up against great resistance. Yet we should not be too discouraged. Jesus himself tells us that this is 'normal' in at least some people. It is not that we are necessarily doing things wrong or letting him down. It is that any worthwhile Christian growth happens against a background of opposition and conflict.

How then do we describe and understand this conflict? In classical Christian thought the opposition is described under three headings in the words used at every baptism service. At the signing of the cross, the congregation say together: 'Fight valiantly under the banner of Christ against sin, the world and the devil and continue Christ's faithful soldier and servant for the rest of your life.' It is to this threefold battle against sin, the world and the devil that we now turn our attention.

Sin

According to the Bible, each one of us is born with a sinful nature. Our natural inclination is to love ourselves rather than to love God and our neighbour. That sinful nature may be partly held in check by the laws and customs of the society in which we live – but left to ourselves we would please ourselves. We incline towards selfishness and evil in our actions, in our words, in our thoughts and imagination and in our attitudes.

Before a person becomes a Christian this sinful nature reigns unchallenged in his or her life apart from the constraints of upbringing and the wider society. The power of sin is such that whole areas of thinking, speech and conduct will be out of all control once a person reaches adult life. It will be impossible for an individual to be free from being driven by lust or ambition, impossible to stop swearing, boasting or gossiping and impossible to break the habit of theft, deception or violence. In many people the power of sin overrides, in time, even their God-given conscience which gradually hardens.

When a person comes to Christ the reign of sin over their life is broken. Through faith in the death of Jesus on the cross all past sins are forgiven. The control and power of the sinful nature to direct every part of a person's life unchallenged is broken and destroyed. He or she is given the gift of a new nature and becomes, in St Paul's words, a new creation.[2] God gives to each new believer the gift of his Spirit to work within us and transform our lives.

Although the power of the sinful nature is broken, however, the sinful nature itself does not disappear but remains as what Paul calls the 'old man'. A struggle begins between the old nature which remains and the new nature God has given. A person who becomes a Christian will often notice significant changes within himself in the first few months of the Christian life. In particular, many testify to the fact that their conscience has come to life again; things that previously did not trouble them are now considered to be wrong. Some people are given the gift of an instant change in certain areas of speech, thinking or behaviour. Some men I have known have instantly stopped swearing – almost without trying – once they have reached that point of commitment and surrender to Christ. Along with a conscience which is growing in sensitivity will come a desire to live a better life and to do what God requires. All of these things are part of the new nature which God gives.

But the old man (or woman) is still strong in us – and will remain so until we are finally with the Lord. Paul described in Romans 7 the battle and conflict which takes place within him and looks forward to the time when he will be finally set free. 'I do not understand what I do. For what I want to do I do not do, but what I hate I do. As it is, it is no longer I myself who do it but it is sin living in me.'[3]

In Galatians 5 Paul describes in graphic terms the battle between the Spirit working within us and the old sinful nature. He spells out honestly the results in human living of letting the old sinful nature control our lives and in contrast describes the fruits of the Holy Spirit: love, joy, peace, patience, kindness, goodness, faithfulness, gentleness and self-control.[4]

All Christians in Key Stages 1 and 2 will experience this battle against sin. In Key Stage 2 it is especially important to give some teaching in this area. The first initial enthusiasm for the Christian life may well be fading. The most obvious results of slavery to the sinful nature have been overcome. The Holy Spirit now begins to work in a deeper way in each person's life to bring out lasting fruit. Yet there may now be greater resistance to change. How are we able to help each other in this battle against sin?

Teaching about baptism

It is vital that new Christians are fully instructed about baptism – even if they are not to be baptized by immersion. Baptism is the great Christian sacrament or sign of new beginnings. As an adult is baptized by full immersion this is not only the symbol of being completely washed and made clean from past sin through the cross. It is also the most powerful symbol of the old self and the old nature being put to death and of the individual rising again with Christ.[5] The radical difference between the old life and the new is affirmed and recognized by this major event of initiation. In preparation for baptism the candidates need to be taught very clearly about this change in their nature – teaching which needs to be expanded and developed and reinforced in Key Stage 2 of their Christian life.[6]

In the months or years after our commitment to Christ we may find that either we fall back into old ways and the sinful nature gains control again or that some significant sin comes to dominate and control our lives. I have known people controlled in this way by jealousy, anger, lust, ambition, pride and a range of other things. Their whole Christian lives have been ruined by actions and a character flowing from one poisonous root. In these instances, where one sin has been allowed to take back the throne, as it were, it is important that the sin is confessed and renounced (see below). I have also found it very helpful to take people back to their baptism and to the idea of the old self being put to death. Paul writes, again in Galatians: 'I have been crucified with Christ. It is no longer I that live but Christ who lives in me'. After a prayer of confession and renouncing sin I have often led the person in a prayer which brings that part of themselves to the cross to be crucified with Christ and to die. Following that kind of prayer there has often been a sense of freedom and of new beginnings in a particular area of the Christian life.

The importance of the will

God has given us a new nature. The old sinful nature and the Holy Spirit are opposed to each other and there is a conflict within us. Yet God does not take away our free will. It matters a great deal which side our own will takes in the conflict. If we persistently choose to side with our sinful nature against the Holy Spirit then we will find ourselves falling back again and again into old ways and coming under the control of sin. If we align our own will with the Holy Spirit's work in our lives then we will find ourselves, albeit slowly sometimes, growing in freedom and in the fruits of the Holy Spirit. Growth in the Christian life in this area is not a passive event which just happens as we grow older in years. As with most things we choose to grow and to develop and to overcome in the battle against sin.

One thing new Christians need to be taught about is themselves: what elements are part of a Christian character. One of the elements there is most need for some to learn about is that they have been given free will to make decisions. Most new Christians also need teaching and guidance in using that free will to make the right decisions.

Confession

As part of keeping watch over each other we are encouraged to 'confess your sins to each other and pray for each other so that you may be healed'.[7] In talking with new Christians over the years I have become more and more convinced of the value of the practice of the confession of sins to another person. Although this can be a ministry which Christians exercise for one another, I believe it is better if the confession is to a recognized Christian minister. First, a recognized minister will have some experience (and grace) in hearing confessions both in respect of confidentiality and being able to deal with what is shared. Second, he or she will normally have been given authority by their particular denomination to declare the forgiveness of sins – as is the case for those ordained priest in the Church of England.

Many people's picture of confession is the regular and frequent visit to the cubicle in the corner of the church by Roman Catholic Christians either remembered from childhood or witnessed on the small screen.[8] In practice, making a confession is often much better as a relaxed, face-to-face affair. I have found it helpful to suggest it to people especially in the following situations:

(a) **When a person becomes a Christian**

When a person comes to faith in Christ as an adult in the 1990s they will often have a number of very significant sins on their conscience. Confession serves as a way of bringing these out into the open, bringing them to Christ, receiving the assurance of forgiveness and, on occasion, some practical guidance on things to avoid in the future. In all these ways the power of sin is broken and the person is set free. For these reasons it has become my practice always to offer the opportunity to make a personal confession to every Christians for Life group in our own church. Only a small number of people in each group take me up on the offer – but for those who do the result is generally very fruitful.

When a person wishes to make a confession near the beginning of their Christian life we would normally meet once for preparation and once, a few days later, for prayer. At the preparation I try to explain clearly just why this will be helpful and what will happen and also encourage the person to prepare carefully by going back over the whole of their life to date and making a short note of particular things they would like to confess. When we meet together to pray, we don't use any set form of prayer (although there are forms available) but, after an initial prayer for grace, I encourage the person to confess the sins on their list (and any others which come to mind) to the Lord, with me as his witness. At the end of the prayer, after a few moments' silence, I pronounce the absolution. It may be that one or two other things have come up which need to be prayed through in a different way – or a small amount of practical help will be needed (but this is not the time for a major teaching or advice session).

(b) **Where there has been a major sin or a drifting away**

Where a person has sinned in a major and particular way as a Christian – such as adultery, or fraud at work – and has this sin particularly on their conscience then, again, it is often appropriate to offer an opportunity for confession. Preparation here may need to be more extensive in talking through the consequences of repentance in terms of making restitution for what is a very recent event and thinking through the mending of relationships. The prayer time itself will focus on the particular sin or event and the circumstances surrounding that. When a person has been a Christian but drifted away and then comes back to an active Christian faith, again, a time of prayer including confession may be very appropriate and helpful. Or when a person has allowed a besetting sin such as jealousy, anger, criticism or gossip to gain a new control over their lives often the best way for the power of that sin to be broken and Christian freedom restored is for there to be a time of confession, combined with the putting to death of the old self described above.

The world

A very honest man once said to me: 'I could never become a Christian. I'd need to find a new way to earn a living.' He was a second-hand car salesman. New Christians need to learn to fight against sin – essentially an internal battle against the old nature. However, they also need to learn how to withstand the pressures of 'the world' which come from outside themselves. Paul writes to the Christians in Rome: 'Do not conform any longer to the pattern of this world but be transformed by the renewing of your mind.'[9] In other words, don't let the world squeeze you into its mould. Be different and be distinctive. Often that will involve conflict.

Modern evangelical Christians often fail here. We have been rightly accused of developing a bolt-on Christianity. Christian worship, prayer and beliefs are simply bolted on to whatever view of the world we already have rather than becoming the lens through which we see the whole of life. So it is that a person can become a Christian and an active member of their local church but never allow their faith to allow them to influence family relationships or work practices, hobbies and interests or the way they vote.[10]

The first step in withstanding the pressures of the world is simply to realize that we are called to be different. We are citizens of heaven and called to be always strangers and pilgrims here. Like salt, our call is to be distinctive from the people around us, not to merge, chameleon-like into the background.

From the world around us come the pressures to spend and try to buy happiness, to seek power for its own sake, and to adopt certain standards and values in human relationships and business practices. From our culture comes a more insidious group of beliefs which are harder to recognize: moderation in all things (when Christ calls for absolute commitment); miracles can't happen in an age of science (when the Bible witnesses to the miraculous as part of the Christian life); people are not interested in religion any more (when they clearly are).

New Christians need to be helped and enabled in the vital task of building a Christian world-view. This happens, in Paul's view, through the renewing of the mind: through clear teaching and preaching which is not afraid to tackle difficult and sensitive issues from a biblical perspective. Too many churches limit their preaching to the safety zone of Christian doctrine and devotional life. We need more engagement in Christian books and preaching with issues modern Christians have to grapple with every day.

Throughout Church history, Christians have made two equal and opposite mistakes in relating to the non-Christian or post-Christian cultures around us. On the one hand we fail to be distinctive from that culture. The salt loses its saltiness; the power to flavour and to preserve. If we do that, Jesus says, as a Church we are good for nothing. On the other hand we withdraw and fail to be involved in that world. The salt stays at the edge of the plate. We forget that God loves his world with passion even though it can be a complex and difficult place for the Christian to live. Throughout Church history the groups of Christians who have been good at being distinctive have been bad at becoming involved, withdrawing instead to a safe and holy huddle. The groups which have been good at being involved have been bad at being distinctive. Where the two come together there really is the potential for God's people to become agents of change in his world.

The devil

'Be self-controlled and alert', writes Peter, 'for your enemy the devil prowls around like a roaring lion seeking someone to devour. Resist him, standing firm in the faith, because you know that your brothers throughout the world are undergoing the same kind of sufferings.'[11]

The picture is one of a flock of goats or sheep. The lion prowls around the edge of the flock in the darkness looking for the wounded, the weak, the wanderers and the stragglers. When an animal becomes separated from the flock the lion pounces and devours him. Christians are called in their baptism to do battle not only against a sinful nature within and the forces of the culture around them but also against the devil: a personal and spiritual force for evil in the universe. In equipping new Christians for this battle we need to be sure that they receive, over the first few years of their Christian life, teaching and instruction in the following areas.

The devil is real

Jesus encountered his testing and temptations and so will we. C.S. Lewis' dictum on the devil has never been bettered. Humanity, he writes, falls into two equal and opposite errors. Either we refuse to believe in the devil at all or we give him too much attention.[12]

The pressure faced from sin and the world in the Christian life is fairly constant from week to week and month to month. Yet anyone who is serious in their discipleship will soon become aware of a different kind of pressure and temptation which is not constant and similar but which keeps on shifting and changing as if attempting to find the weak points in our own defence. It is behind this kind of shifting, personal and strategic attack that we can discern clearly the hand of Satan.

The methods the devil uses to tempt us and distract us will vary according to the time, the place and the person. There is often a great deal of spiritual conflict and temptation around the time a person first becomes a Christian. For many of the people in our own church, life does not become easier when they come to faith. It becomes a great deal more difficult. Sometimes a person will face increased pressure or difficulty at work; sometimes great opposition at home; sometimes there will be periods of illness in the family. There is a danger in becoming over-spiritual and seeing the devil's hand in every little thing which happens. But there is also a danger of being 'under-spiritual' and not becoming aware at all of the spiritual battle and that different strategies and tactics may be used to prevent a person coming to faith and becoming well established in a local church.

Once that 'settling down' has happened it's wise to expect a further period of spiritual conflict, opposition and temptation when a new Christian man or woman begins to take an active part in ministry in and through the local church – especially (we have found) if that ministry involves evangelism and witness. Several years ago my colleague and I eventually became very hesitant about even mentioning people's names in connection with our evangelism programme. It seemed that as soon as we did – or as soon as people began to be involved in outreach – all kinds of things began to go wrong in their lives and they became subject to a number of very difficult spiritual attacks in areas of health, relationships, personal lives or home. A similar thing would happen if a person gave a public testimony in church to what God had done in their lives. The answer to the opposition was not (of course) to abandon our evangelism programme but to develop effective means of prayer support for those taking part, especially for those who are fairly new Christians. We now try to ensure that each person who shares in this or other 'front-line' ministries has at least two people committed to pray for them and for their family regularly. Too often churches place new Christians into the front line of spiritual conflict without giving them the correct support, preparation or equipment for the battle.

The third area where a particular and focused spiritual attack will come in Key Stage 2 of a person's Christian life is during a time of spiritual weakness and wandering – the scenario described by Peter at the beginning of this section. The enemy's chief strategy is to separate the new Christian from other believers and eventually from God. To that end, we have observed, the devil will do all he can to prevent new Christians from building up good disciplines of worship. Once these are established he will try to erode them, little by little. Once the sheep has been separated from the flock it becomes an easy matter to render his or her discipleship ineffective and eventually to persuade new Christians that their time at church was just another phase. After all, you can always go back to it one day. . .

The fourth and final area which is the devil's special tactic, often in Key Stage 2, is the area of false accusation. The word Satan means 'accuser'. The devil is called in Scripture 'the accuser of the brethren'.[13] He will be doing all he can in the first few years of a person's Christian life to undermine any sense of confidence in Christ and sense of value to God. This will happen most often through whispered accusations – reminding the person of fault and failure and past sins. Unless it is effectively countered, such a campaign will often cripple a person's confidence in Christ and in God's love for them. For this reason every Christian needs to be shown that this kind of opposition will come and shown how to oppose it through using Scripture, following the example of Jesus.

Jesus is stronger

Christians are not dualists. That is to say we do not believe in two equal forces of good and evil battling it out for control of the universe. This will need explaining clearly to most new Christians because so much popular culture in films, science fiction novels and cartoons is based on a dualist view of the universe.

The devil is not immortal or eternal and powerful in the same way that God is. The devil is a part of the creation: a spiritual being who has rebelled against God's authority. Through the death of Jesus on the cross, his power has been broken.[14] In these 'last days' (from the resurrection of Jesus until he comes again) the devil has only limited power and is in retreat. He has no claim on or power over a life which has been surrendered to Jesus. He has power only to tempt and test the people of God within their capacity to resist.[15] The promise of Scripture is sure: 'Resist the devil and he will flee from you.'[16]

Often people will come to Christ suffering from a direct, spiritual oppression of some sort caused by what the Bible calls a demon or evil spirit. This is not 'possession' as described in popular films (which is extremely rare). At some time in the past the individual concerned has opened doors in his or her life to the enemy either through some occult activity or through a persistent sin, most commonly of a sexual kind. This oppression may come to light when a person first becomes a Christian or may be dealt with sovereignly by God without it coming to light at all. However, it may not be dealt with then, for different reasons, and may surface in a number of different ways over the next few years as a block and obstruction in the Christian life. The local church will need to develop a ministry of deliverance, alongside a counselling ministry, in any situation where people are coming to Christ from a non-Christian background as adults.[17]

We are equipped for the battle

It will be obvious from what has been said so far that each new Christian needs to be helped in understanding the battle and also needs to be equipped for the fight. One key passage of Scripture in this context is Ephesians 6:10–20 where Paul describes not only the nature of the battle but the armour God gives for the conflict. Somewhere in Key Stage 2 of their journey new Christians need to be introduced to and equipped with the whole armour of God; to learn how to put it on and to use it and be trained for the battle. The belt of truth, the breastplate of righteousness, the shoes of the Gospel, the helmet of salvation, the shield of faith and the sword of the Spirit are vital to Christian discipleship. In these ways and other ways each of us can be equipped to fight valiantly under the banner of Christ against sin, the world and the devil and (we pray) remain Christ's faithful soldier and servant until the end of our lives.

Study Guide

For Ministers and Church Leaders

Questions for reflection and discussion

1 Make a list of people who have dropped away from faith in the past year in your own church. Beside each name write down whether the cause of their falling away was either:

(a) A battle with sin, the world or the devil

(b) A lack of care by the church

(c) You have no idea of the reason

Is there anything you can reasonably do to draw these people back? What lessons can be learned for the future?

2 Review what happens in your own situation in the following areas of ministry and practice:

(a) Adult baptism and those who have been baptized as infants

(b) The opportunity to make a confession

(c) Ministry of deliverance for those who are new to the faith

What is the next step for you in each of these areas?

3 Does the phrase 'bolt-on Christianity' describe the faith of new Christians in your church? What areas of teaching are needed most urgently to help new Christians to develop a different world-view?

Ideas for sermons and training courses

1 A sermon series on 'Sin, the World and the Devil' taking two weeks on each.

2 An expository series on Romans 6, 7 and 8.

3 A mini-conference or midweek training course on spiritual warfare.
4 A series of talks, sermons or services on developing a Christian world-view.

For further reading

C.S. Lewis, *The Screwtape Letters*, Fount, 1959.
Michael Green, *I Believe in Satan's Downfall*, Hodder & Stoughton, 1976.
Romans and Galatians.

TRACK TWO

For Group Leaders

UNDERSTANDING THE OPPOSITION

Introductory exercise

Ask people to share in small groups of three the main struggles they have had since they first became a Christian. You may need to give one or two examples yourself here to set the ball rolling. Briefly pool the answers on a large piece of paper.

Sin, the world and the devil

Beginning with the phrase from the baptism service, summarize the main teaching from the chapter about the battle with sin, the world and the devil. There is no need to go into the detail of how to pray through different things – the main outline will be enough. If you can, draw a chart or visual aids to illustrate what you say. Try and restrict your use of the Bible to one passage in each section. I would suggest Romans 7:15–25 (on sin); Romans 12:1–2 (on the world); Ephesians 6:10–20 (on the devil).

What you are saying may be new to many in the group. Stop after each section and allow time for buzz groups and questions. Encourage people to discover how what you are saying relates to their own lives and spiritual experience.

Bible study

Look at Ephesians 6:10–20 in more detail. Ask group members to make a list of the elements in the armour of God – you may want to provide them with a table to complete. Ask them to think as well about how each piece of the armour may be useful. Again, if you can produce one, a drawing or model of a fully armed Roman soldier would be helpful.

Prayer exercise

A meditation on the whole armour of God. After a few moments of quiet together and an introductory prayer ask the group to imagine that they are going out from here to a fierce battle. Ask them to picture in different ways the conflicts they will face against sin, the world and the devil.

Then ask them to imagine they are putting on piece by piece the whole armour of God. List the parts of the armour as you lead the meditation and perhaps say something about each one. End the meditation with a time of open prayer in the whole group around the theme of standing firm in the battle.

TRACK THREE

For Those Working One-to-One

Review

Review how things have been since your last session together and look especially at any areas of problem or struggle.

Sin, the world and the devil

Share together the material in the chapter under these headings. It may be appropriate to share in some depth the advantage of personal confession to a recognized minister. To focus the study use the same passages as in Track Two. End with a more detailed Bible study of Ephesians 6:10–20.

Prayer together

Especially around any current areas of struggle or difficulty.

TRACK FOUR

For Those Working on Their Own

Daily Bible readings

Mon: *Romans 6:1–14*
Tue: *Romans 7:14–25*
Wed: *Romans 12:1–21*
Thurs: *Galatians 5:16–26*
Fri: *Ephesians 2:1–10*
Sat: *Ephesians 5:1–13*
Sun: *Ephesians 6:10–20*

Longer exercise

Look back over your life and make a list of the things you have done wrong and which you need to confess to God. Include thoughts, words and attitudes as well as actions. Use a separate piece of paper, not your journal, for this list.

Then either make your own private prayer of confession aloud to God in the privacy of your own room. After your prayer read Psalm 103. Or arrange a time to meet with your minister to make a confession to him (or her) and to talk generally about the way your spiritual life is developing.

NOTES

1 Matthew 7:13
2 2 Corinthians 5:17
3 Romans 7:15
4 Galatians 5:16–26
5 Romans 6:1–14
6 The Church of England, rightly in my view, practises the baptism of children of Christian parents and holds firmly to the belief that baptism into Christ can take place only once in a person's life and experience. There is, however, a great need to apply the truth of death and resurrection in baptism to a person's life after they have made an adult profession of faith.

7 James 5:16

8 In practice, the sacrament of reconciliation in the Roman Catholic Church has been changing since Vatican II and is often a face-to-face encounter and a time for spiritual guidance as much as formal confession.

9 Romans 12:2

10 See especially an article by Robert Warren in *Anglicans For Renewal*, August 1993.

11 1 Peter 3:8–9

12 Preface to *The Screwtape Letters*, Fount.

13 Revelation 12:10

14 For further input on this subject see Michael Green, *I believe in Satan's Downfall*, Hodder and Stoughton

15 1 Corinthians 10:13

16 James 4:7

17 See the section on deliverance in *Growing New Christians*, p. 199.

Part Two

Helping Christians to Grow to Maturity

five

Growing in Faith

Now faith is being sure of what we hope for and certain of what we do not see.[1]

How many Christians are growing in faith? My answer is very few. Faith is one of the great growth gaps in the Church. Turn back for a moment to the star-grid in Chapter 2 which tries to show that we need to grow as Christians in several different directions. Then think about some of the Christians you know. It's not, perhaps, too difficult to think of people who are growing in knowledge. I can think of several instances of folk growing in their commitment to church, in personal devotion, in their Christianity influencing daily life and even in the way they encounter God. But it's much harder to think of new Christians in Key Stage 2 or 3 who are growing in the strength of their belief.

If you were to draw a graph of how most people's faith develops it would probably look something like Figure 1. Before a person becomes a Christian their level of faith in God will be somewhere in the range of the society around them. Then, right at the beginning of their Christian life, faith often soars: 'I've met God and he can do anything.' There is a strong sense of God being there, of him answering our prayers and of his plan for our lives. The faith level of a new Christian in Key Stage 1 will often be much higher than the faith level of the church they join or of the person who led them to Christ. It's one of the reasons why newer Christians can be very effective in drawing others to faith.

It's after the first few months that the decline in faith often begins. Maybe we hit a few disappointments either in our faith

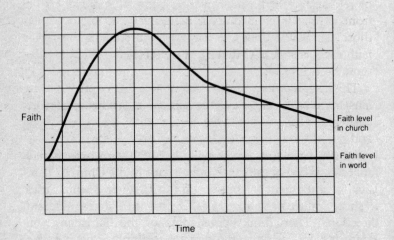

or in our lives. Maybe we just learn from the Christian culture around us. Perhaps the doubts and questions we have are not answered properly. In either case the strength of our faith begins to fall through Key Stage 2 until it reaches the level of the Christians and the church around us. That level itself is not much greater than the level of faith in the world. There our faith will remain for the rest of our Christian lives. We have such a low confidence in God and such a low expectation of what he is able to do. That low assurance of God's goodness and love and ability to act in his world paralyses our Christian lives and paralyses the Church.

This pattern ought not to be the norm. Every new Christian needs to be equipped to grow in faith. One of Jesus' main concerns in bringing the disciples to maturity was to extend and stretch their faith much more than their knowledge. He called them to be different from the world around them in the quality of their believing. He invented a special nickname or rebuke for them: 'men of little faith'.[2] He draws lessons from all that is happening in his ministry to build faith in those who will lead his Church. He teaches us that if we have faith even as small as a mustard seed we will be able to move mountains for God.

This chapter gives three different areas where new Christians in Key Stage 2 need to grow in understanding, three barriers to faith which people need to know how to overcome and three particular areas of the Christian life where faith needs to grow. Our aim should be to build each other up so that the whole body is growing in faith.

Three points to understand

(1) We are loved by God because of his grace and not our own goodness

Susannah has been a Christian for two years and comes from a very unchurched background. A short time ago she became very upset after a church service. Afterwards she explained that she felt a complete failure in her Christian life: 'Every day I say to God, "I'll do it right today". Every day I let him down. I'm just not good enough to be a Christian.'

Miriam is an older lady – a Christian and part of the church family for many years. We were talking together in a group about being sure of going to heaven when we die. 'Of course', she said, 'we can't be sure of anything – but we hope that the good we've been able to do in this life will outweigh the bad we've done and God will see fit to let us into heaven.'

Susannah and Miriam were both making the same mistake in slightly different ways. It's a mistake God's people have made since the first century. We are not saved or put right with God because of anything we do. We all need to begin from the point that we are sinners, spiritually bankrupt and unable to help ourselves. Jesus died on the cross so that our sins can be forgiven and we can be reconciled to God. We receive God's gift of salvation through repentance and faith. This salvation is never deserved and cannot be earned.

Often a new believer will grasp this truth in the first months of their Christian life and experience the freedom of knowing God's love and forgiveness given freely through Christ. However, as the initial joy dies away, it is very common to move away from faith as the basis of our relationship with God and begin to substitute good works and try to earn God's favour.

In first-century Galatia the new Christians made a good beginning after Paul preached to them. They received Christ through faith and with great joy. Only a short time later other teachers had moved in and were instructing the new converts that, now they were Christians, they must be circumcised and keep the Jewish law.[3] In the modern-day Church new Christians will often be taught a whole new set of laws and rules to adhere to shortly after their conversion. We need to remember that it is by grace that we are saved, through faith.

This is the heart of the Gospel. The person seeking to nurture new Christians to maturity will need to return again and again to this theme in public teaching and private conversations. As we grow in our Christian lives that same truth will need to be rediscovered in different ways. For the new Christian there is a need for constant teaching about assurance, of Christ's acceptance of us as we are and that he will never turn us away. Growing in faith means first and foremost growing in our assurance that we are forgiven sinners.

(2) Our faith is based upon Scripture, reason and encounter

Seven years ago, at the beginning of my ministry at St George's, I used to think that most people become Christians in the way that I became a Christian: by attempting to discover whether or not Christianity is true and by making a decision based on evidence. This may be the way most people become Christians in a university setting or in an area where people have had a lot of formal education. But in urban Britain in the nineties this way to faith is not the norm at all. My own estimate would be that fewer than ten per cent of the adults I have seen come to faith have come through analysing evidence and making a decision based on that evidence. The majority have come through an encounter with God in worship and prayer or at a time of great personal need. That encounter with God has led, time and again, to a deep personal faith and a sense of God's presence which has carried that person through Key Stage 1 of their Christian lives.

However, the person who comes to faith in this way will need to learn very early in their Christian lives that our faith does not only rest on our sense of encounter with God registered through our mind or emotions. If it does then the strength of our faith will dip on days when that sense of

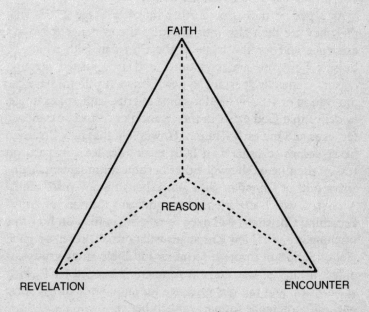

encounter is not as immediate or on days when our emotions are not functioning normally. Our faith rests securely on God's revelation of himself in Scripture, supported by evidence for the existence of God and the truth of Christian faith outside Scripture as well as on the reality of our own encounter with God.

For the majority of new Christians, the single most important support for faith and means of growth in Key Stage 1 will be their own sense of encounter with God. There is such a radical difference from what has gone before. It is very important that new Christians move out from here and come to know God through Scripture as well as in their own experience and in public worship. That is why a wise and sensitive introduction to Bible reading is so important. If that can happen on a one-to-one basis, so much the better.[4]

As a person moves on further into Key Stage 2 it is vital that they are then also introduced to the evidence for God's existence and for the truth of the Christian faith which lie outside Scripture and encounter and are grasped through reason. Generally speaking, a new Christian will not have the motivation or see any need to come to grips with, for example, evidence that God exists in the creation or historical evidence for Jesus and the early Church. However, if that new Christian never comes to grips with faith resting, at least in part, on reason then he or she will either become a fundamentalist or 'grow out' of Christian faith altogether in a few years' time.[5] A church which experiences a significant number of adults becoming Christians will need to reflect carefully on how this teaching is given. New Christians will normally receive a good diet of Scripture through sermons and Bible study groups. A different kind of learning environment is needed for looking at historical and rational evidence for faith; a teaching course or mini-conference format is much better.[6]

For those whose journey into faith does not begin with encounter with God but with faith deduced from reason there will need to be a corresponding broadening in Key Stage 2, but this time in the opposite direction: discovering God not only through evidence in creation and history, but also in Scripture and through direct encounter.

(3) Faith involves action as well as assent

Christian faith is not passive and inactive. Declaring 'I believe and trust in him' should say something about our lives as well as our doctrine. On many occasions when speaking with someone who is on the journey to faith I have used the illustration of a bridge.

Imagine you are walking in the mountains and want to cross a steep gorge. Suspended across the gorge is a rope bridge. You would be wise, before you set foot on the bridge, to examine it from every angle you can. Are the ropes sound? Are they secured to strong supports at both ends? Will the wooden slats on the bridge support your weight? If you can, you will watch other people of your height and weight walk across the bridge to the other side as see them get there safely. You may even put one foot gingerly on the bridge, keeping the other on the mountainside, to test what it would be like to cross.

For the past few months you've been looking into the Christian faith in every possible way. In the picture, you've been examining the bridge. Sooner or later you need to decide whether or not you will place your whole trust in Christ. Placing your trust in Christ means much more than standing on the bank and saying 'I believe that bridge is solid and will bear my weight'. That is not what the Bible means by faith. What the Bible means by faith is walking across the bridge to the other side. For the Christian the word 'faith' means action as well as belief.

This means that to grow in the depth of our faith in God is to grow in the things that we do in him and for him and for others because of him. Action is always a part of faith.[7] To grow in the depth of our belief affects the whole of our lives and character.

Three barriers to overcome

(1) Doubt

All Christians experience times of doubt. For new Christians in Key Stage 2 this will especially be the case. The initial period of joy at the beginning of their Christian life is fading. They are beginning to discover the real cost and challenge of following Jesus and beginning to see the faults and cracks in their fellow Christians and in the Church. The doubts and unanswered questions which were swept aside a few months ago in a great surge of faith begin to surface again and now need to be faced and answered. How are we to equip new Christians to deal with doubt?

Step one is to ensure that we build an environment in which doubts can be voiced and questions openly asked not only for those on the road to faith but for those who have been Christians for some time. There are churches – and groups within churches – where it is considered a major error to ask a searching question. This can be because such a question may shake other people in their faith or because to say such things at all is a sign of spiritual immaturity (and, of course, we all want to be considered 'mature'). The result is that doubts are quickly suppressed and driven underground in a person's own life. Simply to have an honest question is seen as a sin. Doubts which are driven underground in this way do not go away. They simply grow quietly in the darkness undermining faith until, in some cases, it collapses altogether. It is far better that questions are asked and doubts shared and that this process is both encouraged and affirmed in the church and that new Christians are given time.

Step two is to deal with questions that are asked honestly and simply but thoroughly. Again, this cannot always be done effectively within a group setting. I would question the long-term wisdom of encouraging those who are in the second key stage of Christian growth to take part in evangelism-nurture groups.

Generally speaking, questions now need to be asked and answered in a much deeper way and that usually means talking one-to-one. A helpful answer to one person's question may be dull, distracting or confusing to another. The number and type of questions will vary from one person to the next. One man in our own church kept a small notebook in which to write down his questions and ask the clergy for an answer. He would tick them off when he received a satisfactory answer and enjoy the times when we were stumped. Eventually the small notebook was full and his wife bought him a much larger one for Christmas.

Step three is to be aware that much deeper things may lie behind intellectual questions and doubts. I wonder how much real doubt lay behind Thomas' refusal to believe and how much his feelings and remarks were a result of feeling left out, of missing out on the action and of feeling guilty because he was elsewhere?[8] Doubts and questions will often be genuine and need genuine answers. However, they can sometimes be a cover or an excuse for an unresolved emotional need or for sin and guilt or for refusing to respond to God's call. As in every other area of pastoral work, it is so important to learn to listen well and to explore behind a question before rushing in with the theologically correct answer. Questions such as: 'What makes you say that?' or 'How do you feel about that?' or 'How long has that been a problem to you?' or 'Can you give me an example?' will help to draw out any hidden agendas behind the doubt or confusion.

Last of all, Step four, once the question has been resolved, is to draw the person back from unbelief to faith. This is what happens in Jesus' encounter with Thomas. The Lord's command to his disciple is 'Stop doubting and believe'. In any period of intellectual questioning and doubt we step back from faith and from whole-hearted commitment to following Christ. It is one thing to have that question and doubt resolved to our own satisfaction (or to decide that it cannot be resolved but need not affect our faith). That is to stop doubting. But it is quite a different thing to step back into whole-hearted Christian commitment once our faith has been badly shaken. That is what it means to believe. We can usually find many excuses to delay that commitment or make it less than it was.

As a Church, especially as the Church of England, we go too far in promoting doubt. It is good to stimulate debate and to have an environment where questions can honestly be asked and answered. However, the Bible is constantly urging us to move from doubt to faith; to placing our trust again, whole-heartedly, in the promises of God. 'Faith is being sure of what we hope for and certain of what we do not see.' Nowhere in Scripture is anyone commended for hedging their bets or sitting on the fence. If we have doubts, we need to explore them and seek to have them answered rather than become comfortable in living with them and so compromise our discipleship.

In leading a person back to this position of whole-hearted commitment after a significant period of doubt it will often be helpful to pray with them. Faith is a grace given by the Holy Spirit. It is no bad thing to pray for that gift for particular individuals. Just as individual prayers of confession can be helpful in dealing with sin, so a renewal of baptismal vows can be very significant as an individual steps back again into wholehearted discipleship. Good use can also be made of times when the whole congregation together renew these vows, as on Easter Eve in many Roman Catholic and Anglican churches, or times of commitment and dedication, as in the Methodist Covenant Service. On a less dramatic, week by week scale, saying the creed together in public worship is an opportunity to renew faith and commitment just as joining in the general confession is an opportunity to confess our sins together. In many less liturgical Anglican churches, congregations are not as used to reciting the creed as once they were and so miss out on this regular opportunity for affirming both belief and commitment as part of Sunday worship.

(2) Fear

Fear is a very deep part of the human condition without Christ and is real in us all. In the Garden of Eden story, man's first words to God after he has eaten the forbidden fruit are 'I heard you walking in the garden and I was afraid. . .'[9] Over and over again as God speaks to his people in Scripture to

---

BUILDING FAITH THROUGH DOUBT

---

1 Build an environment and a relationship where questions can be asked.

---

2 Deal with questions that are asked in an honest and simple way.

---

3 Be aware of deeper personal issues behind doubts and questions.

---

4 Draw a person back from doubt to faith. It may be helpful to:
 (a) Pray for the grace of faith
 (b) Lead a person through a renewal of baptismal vows

---

call them or commission them he commands them not to be afraid.[10] In almost every case there is a close connection between fear and faith.

We have seen that there are two dimensions to what the Bible calls faith. The first is assent in the mind, heart and will. The enemy of that first dimension is doubt. The second dimension is action leading on from that assent. Fear is the enemy of this action. When God calls Moses to lead his people out of slavery, Moses has no problem whatever with assent: he can see the bush burning, he can hear God's voice and he can see signs and wonders happening before his eyes. What keeps him from the action so that he offers excuse after excuse for not accepting the commission is fear.[11] When the spies go out to explore the promised land and return and report to the people what holds the people back is not doubt – they have had all the demonstrations they need of God's power to save. What holds them back and destroys their faith is fear.[12] When Joshua is commissioned by the Lord and by the people to lead the conquest of the promised land the command he receives from both God and the people is 'Be strong and courageous'.[13]

From the beginning of a person's Christian life we can expect that God will call them out into new situations. However, in the early years of learning and nurture, these will probably not be too stretching or demanding. We may even need to speak words of caution rather than encouragement to step out. Once new Christians begin to come to maturity, however, we should expect that God will challenge them to do some very striking things indeed. Therefore we need to teach people both by word and example not to be afraid to attempt new and bold things for God. We need to teach about the paralysing effect of fear on faith and the whole of life and seek to see people set free from its effects to live for God. Perhaps more than anything else, we should not allow people to become too comfortable in the 'nursery' department of the church, protecting them from the high calling of discipleship. We are not preparing men and women for a lifetime of filling the pews passively taking in sermons but for a lifetime of committed service to Christ, wherever he calls them to be.

Faith is built and fear overcome where people are encouraged to step out and do things for God and see him at work. This is easier done at first as part of a larger group rather than as individuals. A prayer and gift weekend in a church with a target carefully and prayerfully set can lift the level of faith in a congregation and encourage each church member to be bolder in their own walk with God. An evening for enquirers run by a home group can test and stretch faith and build courage and discipleship in every member as people take risks for God. A week spent door-to-door visiting in the parish as part of a team can, once again, stretch and build faith as can sharing in the leadership of a residential camp for children and young people. Nurturing new Christians means looking out for (and sometimes creating) the right opportunities for people to face and overcome fear and to grow in faith.

(3) Suffering

The question of suffering can be an intellectual problem for the enquirer or the new Christian and, if it is not handled correctly, can be a question which eats away at faith. This is the question framed by the person whose life is comfortable at the moment but whose mind is perplexed by the tragedies reported on the news or the ongoing plight of the world's poor.

Answering the armchair doubts of the detached enquirer
may not be easy but it is a very different thing to tackle
questions of faith with a father who has seen his young daughter die of cancer, with a mother whose child is seriously ill,
with a husband whose wife has been unfaithful or with a
woman whose husband has been murdered by terrorists.

Many people may not experience the depth of suffering
which these people passed through – they are all 'real'
examples – but everyone will at some time encounter and
experience life going badly for them; perhaps a prolonged
period of illness or unemployment or real persecution either
in the workplace or the home. Those periods of suffering will
erode faith without the right pastoral care and preparation.
The New Testament letters, which were mainly written to new
Christians, give considerable space to encouraging Christians
who are passing through times of great difficulty. How can
we pass on their lessons to those who are new to the faith?
As with the section on doubt, there are four stages.

Stage one is to prepare the ground properly. That is, we
need to make sure we are giving new Christians a realistic
picture of what the Christian life is like: that it involves suffering as well as joy. Christians are not insulated from the problems which are common to all humanity. God's people cannot
expect to prosper in the midst of recession or be immune
from influenza in winter simply because they are Christians.
Most people who become Christians as adults will have heard
a great many promises of how wonderful the Christian life is
on their way to faith. It will probably come as quite a surprise
to discover that suffering is part of the package; some of it is
even entered into voluntarily.

This preparing of the ground begins with our preaching of
the Gospel. We need to ensure that we are not making promises on God's behalf about freedom from suffering which are
unreal or unbiblical. Our proclamation from the pulpit, in
groups and in conversation needs to give a picture of the
Christian life which is real. Certainly, some forms of suffering
are greatly lessened by becoming a Christian. But Christian
faith is no passport to a pain-free life. If the ground is prepared

in this way, a new Christian will not be unduly surprised when suffering comes or unduly disturbed in his or her faith.

Second, when a person encounters a time of suffering or distress we need to be there to listen and gently to encourage. Again, the listening is far more important than what we say. Often what is needed is not a theological explanation but love and friendship in a time of crisis. It is these which build and restore faith, not complex ideas. Anger with God needs to be expressed in words to a fellow Christian (without us recoiling in shock and horror). It also needs to be expressed in prayer. The psalms of lament serve as models for us as we express the complete range of our own emotions to the Lord who created us. When the pain and the suffering is continuous or very deep then a great deal of time will need to be given to this listening and support. Sometimes this period will last months or even years. During that period a person may or may not attend worship or be part of the ongoing fellowship of the church. We should not abandon them but go on quietly listening and encouraging until the time comes to speak out.

The third stage, when the time is right, is humbly to offer a perspective or an understanding of what is happening. The first part of this may well be to demolish any wrong ideas about God acting through suffering: 'Everything is going wrong in my life; God must be punishing me for something. . .' The second is, in the right way, to demonstrate that, although God does not cause or send suffering, he does put that suffering to use in our lives to build Christian character.[14] It is very common for a new Christian to pass through a time of 'trouble or persecution because of the word' in the first year of their Christian lives. The enemy has a purpose in this time of trouble – to cause the young shoots of faith to shrivel and to die. But God has a purpose in it also: to cause the roots of faith to push down deeper and to build strength and persever-ance. It may be possible to learn practical lessons from particu-lar situations of suffering: where 'persecution' has resulted from a person sharing their faith, has the faith been shared in the most helpful and loving way – or is the new Christian simply making a nuisance of himself by insensitive evangelism? Finally it may be right to point to the many encouragements we receive in the Bible and in Christian literature to rejoice and praise God even in the midst of our suffering and to find blessing there.[15]

Stage four, as with doubt, is to attempt to lead a person right through the time of questioning caused by suffering and back into secure and committed faith in God's goodness. Sometimes it will be necessary to let go of bitterness against other people. Sometimes it will be necessary to let go of bitterness against God himself: to stop blaming God and, as it were, to forgive him. The writers of Psalm 73 have passed through this kind of experience. It is in the midst of worship in the temple that the singer catches a fresh perspective of God's goodness and of his justice, and his faith is restored.

BUILDING FAITH THROUGH SUFFERING

1 Prepare new Christians for suffering of different kinds

2 Listen and encourage

3 At the right time, offer an understanding of what is happening:
   (a) Gently unravel any wrong ideas
   (b) Think through what God is doing in this time
   (c) Consider the Bible's challenge to rejoice in all circumstances

4 Lead the person through suffering and back to faith. This may involve:
   (a) Letting go of bitterness against other people
   (b) Letting go of bitterness towards God

Three areas in which to build faith

Our hope and prayer is to see new Christians go on growing in faith throughout their lives. This means we are praying that they will buck the trend of most Christians and most churches in this country. For this to happen it is vital that we concentrate on building faith in three areas in particular during Key Stage 2:

(1) God has a plan and a purpose for your life

God has that plan and purpose for every individual who comes to faith through our churches. It is much more than to be a committed worshipper in church on Sundays. It is that they should serve him whole-heartedly, seek God's vision for their lives and follow him wherever he leads. When new Christians are given this understanding of God's call on their own lives then faith is able to rise above environment and surroundings in answer to God's call.

(2) God is at work in his world today

There is such a low level of expectancy in so many churches today that God is at work at all. For that reason we need to take special care to build faith in God's involvement and activity today in his Church and in his world. This is done through clear teaching from Scripture and also through drawing attention to actual examples of God at work in human life today either within the local church or on a wider scale. To see God at work builds faith.

(3) God desires to bring revival to his Church

Because faith is at such a low ebb in the Church in the mid–1990s does not mean that it has to be that way. There have been many times in Christian history when God has moved powerfully to bring revival in answer to the prayers and the faith of his people. Every new Christian needs to come to understand this and to pray and have faith that God is able to renew his Church in Britain in our generation and bring a mighty revival to this land.

'Faith is being sure of what we hope for and certain of what we do not see.' In all of our involvement with other Christians, especially those who are near the beginning of their Christian lives, we need to seek to build that kind of faith.

Study Guide

For Ministers and Church Leaders

Questions for reflection and discussion

1 Is the graph in Figure 1 typical of people in your own church? Think through and discuss the reasons why people are not growing in faith.

2 Reflect on your own church in the light of Figure 2. Do you agree that faith should rest on revelation, reason and encounter? Do people come to faith through any one of these more than the others? How do they learn about the other two? What practical steps can you take to address any gaps?

3 Make a note of what you have learned from the section on doubt, fear and suffering. Does anything about your church 'environment' or pastoral practice need to change?

Ideas for sermons and training courses

1 An expository series of sermons on faith covering Romans 5–8, sections of Galatians, Hebrews 11, etc.

2 A mini-conference or teaching series on the obstacles to faith: doubt, fear and suffering.

3 A series of Bible studies on God's calling to individuals in the Old Testament (Abraham, Moses, Joshua, Samuel, etc.) emphasizing God's call to each of us.

For further reading

John Wimber is good on faith generally and especially faith and world-view. See his *Power Evangelism*, Hodder and Stoughton, 1984, Chapter 5.

For a basic review of the evidence for faith see *The Case for Christianity*, Colin Chapman, Lion, 1981.

TRACK TWO

For Group Leaders

Note: there is material in this chapter for more than one session with a group. This is an outline for a single session but you may want to adapt into a series of two or three depending on the needs of the group.

GROWING IN FAITH

Introductory exercise

Look together at the graph in Figure 1 (reproduced on a sheet or OHP). Does this describe the pattern of your own faith? What habits, events or experiences have helped your own faith to grow?

Look at the questions in threes then share your answers with the whole group.

Three things to understand about faith

The importance of faith:
It is through faith that we are put right with God.
Faith rests on revelation, reason and encounter.
Faith involves action as well as assent.

Group exercise: the barriers to faith

In small groups make a list of:

(a) Questions you have which have led you to doubt God
(b) Fears which have prevented you moving forward in faith
(c) Things you or those you love have suffered which have been a barrier to faith

Share your answers in the wider group and spend some time with each section.

An encouragement to grow in faith

The section may need to pick up from the previous exercise or focus on the three growth points for faith mentioned in the chapter.

Prayer exercise

A meditation on Jesus' encounter with Thomas (John 20:24–29).

Take a moment to be quiet and still together. Ask the group to imagine themselves in the upper room: to imagine the sight, sound, smells, taste and touch of what is happening there. Then ask them to imagine the encounter between Jesus and Thomas unfolding as they watch. After that encounter has taken place, ask them to imagine a personal meeting in the corner of the room between Jesus and themselves. Focus especially on Jesus' words: 'Stop doubting and believe'.[16]

TRACK THREE

For Those Working One-to-One

Again, there is material enough for several meetings and conversations here.

Bible study Hebrews 11

Draw out the meaning of faith and the kind of faith displayed by those mentioned in the chapter.

Discussion together

Around the headings in the chapter:
(a) Three things to understand about faith
(b) Doubt, fear and suffering
(c) Three directions for faith to grow.

Prayer together

TRACK FOUR

For Those Working on Their Own

Daily Bible readings

Mon: *Hebrews 11* Heroes of faith
Tue: *Matthew 14:22–33* Peter walks on water
Wed: *John 20:24–31* Jesus and Thomas

Thurs: *Romans 8:28–39* Christian assurance
Fri: *James 2:14–26* Faith and action
Sat: *Psalm 73* Faith and suffering
Sun: *Habakkuk 3* A song of faith

Longer exercise

Either: An extended meditation on Jesus' encounter with Thomas (see Track Two)
or: A time of self-examination: what stops your faith from growing?

Take a page of your journal or a blank sheet of paper and divide it into three columns. Give them the headings Doubt, Fear and Suffering. Write in the first column any unresolved doubt and questions you have about the faith. In the second column make a note of your fears of going forward with God. In the third think through any times of suffering you have passed through and the scars that may have left on your faith.

Then next to each make a note of what you need to do. Perhaps some reading on doubts – or book a session with the vicar. Perhaps some prayer for the fears. Perhaps a need to let go of bitternness for the times of suffering.

End the time of reflection by quietly renewing your baptismal vows (ASB p. 276) or saying the Apostles Creed. You may like to build the creed into your daily prayer time for the next few weeks.

NOTES

1 Hebrews 11:1
2 Matthew 6:30; 8:26; 16:8
3 The whole of Galatians is addressed to this dilemma.
4 David Watson gives an excellent description of his own introduction to the Scriptures through a regular meeting with David Sheppard in his first year as a Christian: *For You are My God*, Hodder and Stoughton, 1983, pp. 24ff.
5 The dangers of growing out of faith are obvious. The dangers of fundamentalism are less obvious but no less real. For a fundamentalist, because faith rests only on Scripture, the Bible has to be upheld as without error in every respect. This means

there is a retreat from any engagement in and with science, historical scholarship and philosophy. The only motive for this retreat is a fear that the foundations of faith will collapse if any of these disciplines can demonstrate that the Scriptures are in error in any way. The result is that reason is suspended leaving the individual Christian in danger of being manipulated by particular interpretations of the Bible and leaving the Church retreating from contemporary culture and debate. One of the key theological tasks for the Church in the 1990s must be the separation of evangelical theology from fundamentalism.

6 There is a shortage of good published material in this area.

7 See James 2:14–26

8 John 21:24–29

9 Genesis 3:10

10 Abraham in Genesis 15:1; Isaac in Genesis 26:24; Moses in Exodus 3:6; etc.

11 Exodus 3

12 Numbers 13 and 14

13 Joshua 1

14 Romans 5:3

15 See Habbakuk 3; Acts 16:16–40; Philippians 1 and 4. Care needs to be taken to ensure new Christians do not slip over from attempting to praise God *in* all circumstances (which builds faith) to praising God *for* all circumstances (which is something close to blasphemy). Books containing the latter teaching have been popular in charismatic Christian circles for some years.

16 This way of leading people in prayer through a Bible passage is based on the Spiritual Exercises of St Ignatius and can be a very helpful way of prayer and listening to God for some people. It should always be introduced to a group with care and with the footnote that some will not find it helpful. If any people believe they hear God saying anything disturbing this should be shared with the group leader after the meeting. For a full introduction to the Ignatian way of prayer see Gerard Hughes' book, *God of Surprises*, Darton, Longman & Todd, 1982.

six

Growing in Worship

Three letters to Mark

(1) On the priority of worship

Dear Mark,

Thanks for your letter. The news that you have become a Christian was very good to receive. Yes, I do remember very clearly all the conversations we had together. I shall enjoy the memory even more now I know that they played a small part in your coming to faith. It's good to hear, also, that you've joined a group for enquirers and new Christians run by the local church. There's going to be a lot of learning and growing to be done over the next few years. The Bible speaks of a new Christian being like a small child. You will certainly need the support of the local congregation around you as you begin to grow.

You ask me what is the most important thing now that you have become a Christian. It's a very good question – but I don't think you have the right answer. Sharing the faith is very important and, as time goes on, you may well prove to have the gift of evangelism. But telling others about Christ, however important that is, should never become the most important thing in our Christian lives (or in the church we are part of). If we are Christians the centre of our lives now should be worshipping God.

There is an old summary of Christian doctrine in question and answer form which asks as its first question: 'What is the chief end of man?' The word 'end' means not just what will happen at the end of our lives but purpose and destiny. The question is asking: what were we made for? The answer comes back: 'The chief end of man is to know God and enjoy him for ever.' A great deal of biblical truth is contained in that short question and answer. Men and women were made to know God and enjoy him for ever. Our chief occupation when we are in heaven will be praising God. As Christians that is to be our prime calling on earth as well: declaring the praises of him who called us out of darkness to his wonderful light.

When a teacher came to Jesus and asked him a similar question to the one you asked me, 'Of all the commandments (that is, of all the things we do for God) which is the most important?' Jesus reply was very clear:

'The most important one is this: "Hear O Israel, the Lord our God, the Lord is one. Love the Lord your God with all your heart and with all your soul and with all your mind and with all your strength." ' (Mark 12:29–30 quoting Deuteronomy 6:4, 5)

The longest book in the Bible, and the first Old Testament book new Christians should read, is the Book of Psalms which teaches us how to praise and worship God for our creation, our salvation and our day-to-day life. Worship is important to us at the beginning of our Christian lives and all the way through for a number of different reasons. Let me try to explore one or two.

First, worship gives us a perspective on the universe and on ourselves. Before we become Christians our lives are largely centred upon ourselves. Worship directs our mind and our lives outward to God's perspective:

> When I consider the heavens and the work of your fingers,
> The moon and the stars which you have set in place,
> What is man that you are mindful of him,
> The son of man that you care for him? (Psalm 8:3–5)

We need to gain that perspective each day of our lives as Christians but we especially need it in the first few years of our life with Christ as we leave behind the old and put on the new.

Second, worship allows us to appreciate and to know and to enjoy God. One of the most helpful ways to think of praising God is to think of the way you enjoy a beautiful painting or a fine piece of music or a good meal or a walk in the country. As we look or listen or taste or walk we continually find new things to delight in and new things to enjoy. It is the same with God. The more we worship him the better we come to know him and the more we discover there is still to explore. The better we come to know him then the more we come to love him.

One of the most common traps new Christians fall into, especially those who are naturally keen and committed, is to get too bound up too early with Christian ministry. It is very exciting to be working for God and doing things for him. It gives us a sense of worth and even, sometimes, of importance. But if we are not careful, what we do for God becomes the centre of our Christian life instead of our relationship with him. We need to be building good habits of worship and of praise in our life before we launch out into ministry.

Third and last, worship opens us out as people. You may have noticed that the natural attitude of people all around you at work and in the pub and sports club is to criticize and to blame. To criticize is the opposite of to praise. As we criticize others, our own world becomes a little more closed and restricted, shutting out the light. As we praise God, we ourselves begin to open out again making it easier to praise others and allowing the light to come in.

Normally in the first few years of our Christian lives, if, like yourself, we become Christians as adults, we find praise very difficult. The habits of a lifetime mean that we have become used to attracting attention, honour and glory to ourselves and pulling others down. We have either enthroned ourselves at the centre of our lives or we have given first place to some idol (our work, or a sport or hobby, a car or a house, or a relationship). As we worship we proclaim again and again that the Lord is King and is enthroned at the centre of our lives. In the words of the Psalms once again:

> Come let us sing for joy to the Lord,
>   Let us shout in triumph to the Rock of our salvation
> Let us come before him with thanksgiving

and extol him with music and song.
For the Lord is the great God,
the great king above all Gods. (Psalm 95:1–5)

It's well worth asking why God places such a high priority on us worshipping him. It is not because he needs our praise or needs anything from us at all. It is simply because to have the worship of the living God at the centre of our lives is to be living as we were designed to live. Human beings will become like whatever they worship. A man who worships money will become narrow and selfish. His life will shrink so that money alone is at the centre and there is room for nothing else. A man or woman who worships the living God will have a joy at the centre of their lives and every other priority will fall into place.

The worship and praise of the living God is the highest calling and greatest adventure a man or woman can have. Without a doubt exploring God in worship is the greatest priority for a Christian in the beginning, middle or end of their Christian life. If you put praise at the centre you will not go far wrong.

Yours in Christ
Steve

(2) On good disciplines of worship

Dear Mark,

Thanks for your reply to my last letter. I'm glad it all made sense and that things generally are going well. I can quite understand that you need some help with how to worship. Most of us do. Let me try to give you a few starters.

Perhaps the most essential starting point is to develop a strong discipline of Sunday worship in your own local church. You are already linked to a church because of Beverley and the group you have joined – so you don't need to spend any time looking round for a suitable one. Now you are a Christian it's time to realize that your place on a Sunday is with your Christian family at worship.

Yes, I know there are lots of other things you have been used to doing on a Sunday including have a bit of peace and quiet while the wife and kids are at church. But there really is no way around this one. If Jesus Christ is Lord of your life now, that means putting him first in the prime time on the first day of the week. You cannot squeeze God into your spare time. Other things will now have to fit around this call to worship. At least you know that you will have the support of your family in this.

I've found over several years of encouraging people to become regular in worship that it's no good beating about the bush on this one. Good habits are about as hard to form as bad ones are to give up. If you've ever tried to give up smoking or to change your diet you'll know what I mean. For that reason it's hardly ever any good to say 'I'll go to church a bit more often now I'm a Christian'. It's just like saying 'I'm going to give up smoking one day soon'. When Sunday comes around there are always ten good reasons why you can wait another week to go to church. You won't begin to form a good discipline of Sunday worship until you simply decide that, on Sundays, church is where you are meant to be – no questions asked.

Next, try and be prepared for worship when you go. A great many other things happen at church on Sundays besides worship. It's where you meet and get to know your Christian family and hear God's word read and explained. It's where you join together with other Christians to pray for the needs of God's world. But giving thanks and praise to God is the main reason we meet together. For that reason we need to give thought to our preparation. If Sunday worship is the centre of our week and the most important time we spend with God, then it seems strange that so many turn up late or just before the start of the service. Surely it's better to aim to be there in good time so as to have a few moments to pray before the service begins? It's better still to have been up in good time and to have prayed at home before making your way to church. It's important to have God at the front of your mind – not what you want to say to Mrs Smith over coffee about last Tuesday's meeting. Be open to what he wants to say to you. Be aware of the different prayers and needs you are bringing to him. Bring to mind the things you want to say thank you for in the week gone by.

It takes time to grow into the rhythms of Christian worship and the different times of the Church's year. You will find some things you can relate to immediately and others which need some explanation. Be patient here. If you can understand everything about your church services in the first few months of going then you can be sure that the worship won't be feeding you and satisfying you spiritually in a few years' time. No doubt there will be some sessions on worship in the group you are attending. If there are some things not explained properly by the end ask for a session with the vicar and take your list of questions to him.

Once a Sunday discipline is established you will need to begin to grow in praise and worship during the week. As an old hymn puts it, our praise is meant to be seven whole days not one in seven. Different people find different things helpful as springboards to worship. If you live in the country – or travel through it regularly – then the creation is a great help to worship. If, like you and me, you spend most of your working life in town and city you probably have to look a bit harder for the creation. Some people find tapes of worship songs very helpful as a way of learning new words to praise God. Most people find the new songs more accessible and intimate in worship than the older hymns, and there's nothing wrong in that. But don't neglect those hymns completely. Their words have been tried and tested by several generations of Christians and they carry truth over from one age to the next. The Psalms are a wonderful quarry for praise, as I mentioned in my last letter. If you haven't started reading them yet then try to make a beginning soon. And for some people – especially those who have hectic lives – the most wonderful help in personal praise is silence and space. Even five minutes snatched in the middle of a busy day can make all the difference.

Worship for the Israelites of the Old Testament and for the Jews in Jesus' day centred around animal sacrifice at the temple. Bulls, goats, pigeons and other animals were offered up at various times by the priests as gifts of love to God or to atone for sin or as a thanksgiving. We are no longer called on to worship God in that way, through animal sacrifice. Jesus himself died for our sins: the one perfect sacrifice. However, our worship is meant to involve far more than our words or even the attitude of our minds. We are called to become living sacrifices to God, in Paul's words:

> Therefore I urge you, brothers, in view of God's mercy, to offer your bodies as living sacrifices, holy and pleasing to God. This is your spiritual act of worship. (Romans 12:1)

Broadly speaking that means that everything we do and everything we are is meant to be offered in worship to God. Worship then becomes a way of life and a way of offering our whole lives to God. It is far more than going to church on Sunday or even directing our minds and hearts to God during the week. You will no doubt find, as the rest of us do, that the main problem with a living sacrifice is that it keeps getting off the altar.

I hope that gives you something to be getting on with in terms of worship.

Yours in Christ,

Steve

(3) On Holy Communion

Dear Mark,

It's been some time since I heard from you and it was something of a relief to get your brief note. I'll do what I can to give you an introduction to Holy Communion from this distance – but you'll need to talk to someone on the ground there as well. First, though, let me deal with your final point.

I was a little bit alarmed to hear that, a year into your Christian life, you had stopped going to worship regularly because you are no longer getting as much from it as you used to. I think you need to be a little careful here. I can appreciate that you may go to church on a given morning and not be able to relate to the sermon, the songs, the prayers or the readings. That's quite a common experience. But it is more an indication of something taking place within you than a measure of the services themselves. Every Christian experiences dry times in worship. They are times when God is stretching and developing our spiritual muscle. The right response to them is not to drop out of worship because there is no immediate payback but to persevere and to grow in discipline. Eventually we will begin to enter into the reality and the joy of worship again.

It all boils down to the question: do we go to church to worship because of our love for God and because he commands it or because we want to 'get something' from the service? If we go for the first (and right) reason then we will simply be there week by week even if the choir is off-key and the vicar is having a bad few months. Often, to our surprise, we will find we come away having gained something from the worship, even though we find it difficult to understand how. As we are faithful to the Lord, so he is faithful to us.

However, if our primary motive is to 'get something' out of the service we will often come away disappointed even if we listen to the most inspiring preaching and music in the world. Why? Because our whole approach to worship has become me-centred and not God-centred. Like the rest of our consumer society we have become concerned for what we can get not what we can give. We go to church on Sundays primarily to give our worship to God not to receive from him. As soon as we focus on receiving then we move from being worshippers to being sermon- and service-critics. In a very short time no preacher or service will satisfy or feed us. We become one of a small army of people who began the Christian life well but who have unchurched themselves by having entirely the wrong focus in worship.

Yes, I grant you, it is important for those preparing worship to make this a high priority and to use imagination and skill in leadership and planning. But in the end, whatever human ingenuity we use, each worshipper needs to come with the right attitude: to worship the Father in spirit and in truth. I hope you don't mind me writing honestly and a little bluntly. You need to come back to your first priorities and your first love. Stop comparing your own church with the one round the corner. Blossom where God has planted you. And return to the simple principle of going to Sunday worship to give your praise to God – no matter what else may be happening in the building.

Learning to worship God through the Holy Communion service is important for every Christian. I suspect many don't appreciate or understand half of the significance of what is happening in the words of the service as the drama unfolds. The words and titles given to the service sum up its meaning. Holy Communion means fellowship with God at a most infinite level. The Lord's Supper means a meal taken with Jesus. Eucharist is a Greek word meaning 'thanksgiving'. The whole service is an offering to God of thanks and praise and celebration, especially for Jesus.

The words of the service (the liturgy) give a structure and framework for worship which are very important. They give balance, depth and meaning to the service. These bare bones of liturgy are then filled out with different songs, hymns, readings and prayers each week. The first half of the service ('The Ministry of the Word') begins with a time of preparation for worship, including confession. It continues with readings from Scripture and, usually, a sermon. A special prominence is given in the Communion service to the gospel reading since the service has Jesus at the centre. After the sermon the whole Christian community join together in affirming our faith and intercede for the needs of the world. We then begin to focus on God's invitation to us in the prayer 'We do not presume'; we celebrate our unity in Christ as we share the peace together (I know it feels strange at first, but most people do get used to it); and we offer our own gifts to God.

The great eucharistic prayer is a thanksgiving to God for all his work in creation, in sending Jesus and in the gift of the Holy Spirit. In the central part we remember again the Last Supper and Christ's death on the cross. We praise God for his wonderful gift of Jesus and we pray that as we share in communion together God will renew us, unite us and inspire us to go out and serve him in the world. We pray together as

Jesus taught us. The priest breaks the bread as Jesus broke it and we come together around the Lord's table.

The bread and the wine have not changed in substance but they have been set aside in the great prayer of thanksgiving. We draw near with faith and in faith we receive the body of our Lord Jesus Christ which he gave for us and his blood which he shed for us. The bread and wine are tokens of his love, signs of his forgiveness and a means of his grace to us. As we receive them we are strengthened and nourished in our walk with him in ways which are beyond our understanding. The old definition of a sacrament is still worth learning: Holy Communion is 'an outward and visible sign of an inward and invisible grace'.

The Bible commends careful preparation before we receive Holy Communion (1 Corinthians 11:28). That certainly includes preparation before we come to worship, during the service itself and as we and others are receiving Holy Communion. It is a holy time – not a time for gossip and chatter as it has become in many churches. As we return to our places we continue to thank God for his love in Jesus. In the final prayers we offer ourselves afresh as living sacrifices to God and we are sent out to be lights for Christ in the world in the week to come.

The service looks forwards in time to when Christ comes again and back to his ministry and death. We look inwards at ourselves and out to the world. It is about my own relationship with God but also about our fellowship together as the Body of Christ. There are echoes of Scripture and tradition in every part of the service. Above all there is a central act of Christian worship here which every Christian can go on exploring and finding new layers of meaning in year by year for the rest of his or her Christian life.

I hope these three letters have been enough to give you a start on worship.

Yours in Christ,
Steve

Study Guide

For Ministers and Church Leaders

Questions for reflection and discussion

1 How would you answer Mark's first question: what is the most important thing in the Christian life? Does this reflect the priorities of your own Christian life and of your own church? What are the consequences for church life of putting evangelism at the top of the list?

2 Do new Christians find it easy to establish a discipline of regular Sunday worship in your own congregation? What teaching do they receive on this? What pressures work against them?

3 Looking back over the last three years – what teaching have any of the congregation had on Holy Communion and on worship generally?

Ideas for sermons and training courses

1 A series of sermons or Bible studies opening up the Psalms as model prayers for praise or lament.

   Note: most sermons and studies of the Psalms still treat them as though they are autobiographical poems by King David – despite a century of biblical scholarship. Try a different approach – and see how much further it takes you.

2 A mini-conference or training course on principles of worship not just for worship leaders but for the whole congregation. You may like to invite members of a neighbouring church to lead it for you.

3 An evening on 'Getting to know your ASB' (for Anglicans). We have a tremendous resource for personal and public worship which so few new Christians get to know.

4 A teaching course or sermon series on Holy Communion.

For further reading

Jubilate by Daniel Hardy and David Ford, Darton, Longman &
  Todd, 1984, is a very stimulating theology of worship and
  praise.
Liturgy and Liberty by John Leach, Monarch, 1989, is an excellent, practical discussion of the ways of combining old and
  new in worship.

TRACK TWO

For Group Leaders

Track two does not deal with worship in Holy Communion.
Take a separate evening over this – possibly inviting someone
who is ordained priest to come and celebrate Holy Communion in the group and explore the service in more depth.

GROWING IN WORSHIP

Introductory exercise

If you had to name the most important dimension to the
Christian life, what would it be?

Answer the question in buzz groups, then pool your
answers. Include some input on the priority of worship from
Letter 1.

Bible study

Break into small groups of three to four people. Each group
should spend a few minutes studying one of the following
psalms and then share their findings with the whole group:
Psalm 8; Psalm 104; Psalm 95; Psalm 150. What does each
psalm tell us about worship and about God himself?

Some principles of worship

Draw out the principles in the second letter of discipline in
Sunday worship (you may need some discussion here), of
praising God day by day (what helps different members of the
group?), and of becoming a living sacrifice.

The principles could lead into a short exposition and encouragement to study Romans 12.

Prayer exercise

A time of thanksgiving and praise to God.

Work in the same small groups as for the Bible study. Each group should work together to produce a psalm of praise and thanksgiving to God. If possible each member of the group should contribute ideas for one of the verses.

Play some quiet music as each group in turn reads their psalm in a time of praise and worship.

TRACK THREE

For Those Working One-to-One

Bible study: *Psalm 145*

Discuss the priority of worship and the different reasons we have for praising God.

Discussion together

Around the principles in the second letter – focusing especially on any difficulties in worship.

Prayer together

TRACK FOUR

For Those Working on Their Own

Focus on the psalms of praise.

Daily Bible readings

Mon: *Psalm 8* The wonder of God in creation
Tue: *Psalm 23* God's care for his people
Wed: *Psalm 46* Security in God's care
Thurs: *Psalm 95* Come let us sing for joy
Fri: *Psalm 103* God's tenderness with his people
Sat: *Psalm 104* God's power in creation

Sun: *Psalm 145* The character of God

Longer exercise

A study of Romans 12.

This chapter explains what it means to be a living sacrifice and to offer our whole lives in worship to God. It is a chapter well worth getting to know.

Begin by reading each section through several times so you have good sense of the meaning and of the passage as a whole. If you can, get hold of a simple commentary on the chapter and read it through.

Then summarize, in your own words, the meaning of each paragraph. In particular make a list of all the commands and instructions in the passage. Mark with a star the ones you need to take particular notice of at the present time.

Finally choose one verse from the passage and meditate on that verse thinking about each word in turn. Make a note of what you believe God is saying to you about offering your life in worship.

seven

Growing in Prayer

Many people pray before they ever become committed Christians. Sometimes their prayer will be limited to 'Help'. Often it will be restricted to intercession for family and close friends, especially in times of crisis. Some have been taught to pray as children either in the home or at school and carry their childhood habits of praying on into adult life. My guess is that fewer people than we think progress beyond this point in growing in their lives of prayer even after they have become Christians and taken their place as active members of a local church – simply because they are not shown how to pray. Those who do progress a little way get stuck a little further down the road because they have not been equipped with the right resources to go on growing and developing a prayer life for themselves.

In Key Stage 1 of their Christian life some people find prayer very straightforward – a two-way conversation with God which they simply slip into whenever they want to. Others will find talking and listening to God the hardest part of their Christian lives. However, by the time most people have reached Key Stage 2 there is usually a need for some extended input on prayer. Even those who began well are now running out of steam and ideas and are in need of some help.

Some basic principles

The first part of the learning and growing is to clear up some common misunderstandings about prayer.

(1) Prayer does not come naturally

We are not born knowing how to pray – any more than we are born knowing how to talk, to listen or to walk. It is one of the things in life we have to learn and learn about. Nor does the gift of being able to pray come automatically when we are born again of the Spirit. Although our relationship with God will be altogether different we still need to be shown how to express that relationship in prayer and how to listen to what God says to us. As someone who has found prayer quite difficult at different times, I've always been enormously encouraged by the disciples' request to Jesus in Luke 11: 'Lord, teach us to pray.' Over the years, that request has become my prayer also and Jesus, in his grace, has become my teacher. When helping other people to pray it has become a first principle for me to introduce them to this particular request so that the Lord becomes their teacher and guide in prayer and not any one individual.

We learn how to pray. Like any other area of learning there are certain things you can learn in advance from someone else or through reading a book. But there are many things you can learn and understand only through experience and reflecting on that experience with others who have passed the same way. It is very important, therefore, from the beginning of a person's Christian life, to encourage them to talk openly about prayer – if possible without guilt or fear so that experiences can be shared openly and new things learned.

(2) Prayer is not just about asking God for things

'God bless Mummy and God bless Daddy and God bless cousin Jack.' For most of us prayer begins with requests. We may hear a lot about intercession in the life of the church and that feeds the impression that the most important part of prayer is asking God for help either for others or for ourselves. Intercession is important, but it is not the heart of prayer.

The heart of prayer is developing the most wonderful relationship of our lives: our relationship with the Father who created us, the Son who redeemed us and the Holy Spirit who gave us life. Intercession – and every other part of prayer – flow out of this developing and growing relationship.

As with any friendship, the key to growing together is quality time spent together regularly. Prayer to the living God can never be reduced to a religious duty or a chore to be completed at the end of a busy day. Finding a time to pray, like allocating time for public worship, means giving God first place and building up good habits. Different people will find different times more helpful than others. Some will be early morning people. Others will pray best in the evenings. But in order to nourish a growing friendship real time needs to be given.

(3) There is no single 'right' way to pray

One of the best principles of prayer is to use what helps you. That is likely to be different in different seasons of your life as well as differing from person to person. However, it does mean that we need to beware of being too prescriptive when helping people to grow in prayer. There is no convenient blueprint that can be followed when helping someone to walk more closely with God. There is great need for discernment, a listening ear and a godly caution in making pronouncements and suggestions. It's much better to say 'You may find this helpful' than to insist 'This worked for me and I'm sure it will work for you'. If it doesn't, a person almost always feels that it is his or her fault.

It's also a feature of our Christian lives that we change as we grow older in the faith and older in years. The questions and searching we bring to our relationship with God change also. That must to some degree affect the way that we pray. Hence the need, not only in Key Stages 1 and 2 but in the whole of our Christian lives to have access to good spiritual direction for every Christian person who wants to grow. This is a particular need at times of transition of faith or life stages.

Establishing a basic framework for prayer

Having given these words of caution, it does seem to me that one of the tasks in helping people to grow in prayer in Key Stage 2 is assisting them to find a helpful basic pattern for prayer within which they can experiment and settle and grow for this first, major period of their Christian lives.

I would always seek to encourage someone starting out on the Christian life to aim to establish a basic discipline of prayer each day of fifteen to thirty minutes. Not many people will be able to keep to this discipline seven days a week. We should do all we can not to set guilt traps for people to walk straight into. But to aim for a daily discipline sets the sights high, which seems to me to be right. The first question someone starting out on this disciplines needs to establish is *'When* is the best time for me to pray?' Some may need help in working through the options. Others can manage this one for themselves. It's always worth warning people that once they set aside a particular time to pray they will almost always meet some spiritual resistance as that time becomes part of the daily routine. It's always worth mentioning that a time for prayer should not be a time when energy is low or you feel like a nap.

The second primary question to be answered is *where* a person intends to pray. Jesus gives clear instructions that prayer should be unseen and in private.[1] Jesus himself often prays out of doors. For the student at university or the person who lives alone or in a large house finding space to pray may not be a problem. But for the person who lives in a family in a fairly small house with not much privacy (and who may be the only Christian in the family), finding space to pray can be a real problem. More than one person I have known has begun to work out a life of prayer locked securely in the smallest room in the house. Like most problems this one can normally be solved but it can help to work it through with someone else.

The third question is *how* to pray. Just exactly how do you spend fifteen to twenty minutes in prayer at 7.00 a.m. in the morning in the back room downstairs before the rest of the family get up? Some people need no help here, especially at the beginning of their Christian lives. They are simply given a tremendous grace of prayer and of friendship with God. Most of us need a framework which includes not only time for prayer but also for personal Bible reading. There are a number of possibilities. In my own experience most people relate well either to a framework based around Bible reading notes or a framework built around the Daily Office.

Building a framework around Bible reading notes

This may be a controversial statement to some: in my view, dated Bible reading notes are not always helpful for new Christians in Key Stages 1 and 2. This advice runs against the received wisdom, especially in evangelical Christian circles. However, most new Christians I have known have not had the self-discipline to have a time of prayer and quiet every day (or even most days) in the first few years of their Christian life. Using dated notes serves as a constant reminder of how much we have failed and how much catching up people have to do. Each time a person comes to the notes they are already several days (or weeks) behind and the dominant emotion at the beginning of a time of prayer is guilt because I haven't spent time with God for six days. A sense of failure and guilt is not the best introduction to a time of prayer. For newer Christians some kind of undated guide to the Bible works better.[2]

The other main danger of using dated or undated notes is that the routine of 'doing the notes' replaces prayer. Most of us will recognize the danger. We have only a limited time to 'have a quiet time' before the next intrusion and appointment. Dust is blown off the Bible and the notes. We look up today and turn to the Bible passage, trying to come to grips quickly with a passage of Scripture. From reading the Bible we turn immediately to reading the notes. 'Prayer' then consists of reading a list of names to God or dashing off a few requests for the day. That's all we have time for. Sorry, Lord, catch you tomorrow. We may have had a quiet time to satisfy our conscience – but we haven't really prayed.

Notes can be a great help as long as they are used as a support for prayer and not a substitute for it. People need to be taught how to use them. One guide is to follow the steps in table 1. Find a time to pray when you really do not have to rush. If you only have five minutes for prayer on a particular morning it's better to spend that five minutes in prayer and forget the Bible reading than to try to do the Bible reading and not have time to make contact with the Lord. At the start of your prayer time take some minutes to prepare for prayer. There are a number of ways to do that. You may find it helpful to listen to some Christian music on tape; to say 'thank you' for the events of the last few days; to read a familiar psalm; or to say sorry to God for anything which is particularly on your conscience. Preparation in prayer, as in most things, is essential. We cannot expect to simply rush into the presence of the Lord of heaven and earth.

A PRAYER TIME BASED AROUND BIBLE READING NOTES

1 *Preparation:* Thanksgiving; confession; praise and worship; silence; ask God to speak to you through his word.

2 *God's word:* Read the passage several times. Chew it over. Try and catch what God is saying to you.

3 *The notes:* Read them and take note of anything which strikes you. Then go back and read the passage again.

4 *Intercession or thanksgiving:* According to the pattern you develop (see below).

After that time of preparation look up the passage set in the notes for today. Before you read, ask God to speak to you through his word. Then read the passage – not once but several times. You may like to make a note of anything you don't particularly understand to come back to at a later date. Try and prevent your prayer time becoming an academic Bible study. As you read the passage, listen to what God is saying to you. A particular verse may strike you – or even a word in a verse. There may be a lesson for your own life or for a situation you will face today. Only after you have spent a little time listening to God through his word should you read the notes – otherwise these become a short cut and make us lazy. Take what is valuable from the notes for the day, perhaps reading the passage again. Then move on into a time of intercession or thanksgiving arising from the passage or based around a pattern you normally use.

Building a framework around a Daily Office

A close friend of mine, who was a lay reader in the church, struggled with prayer for years. She simply couldn't pray and spend time with God each day. The words wouldn't come. After trying a number of different ways, without success, she began praying using the service of Morning Prayer from the Alternative Service Book. All of a sudden it was all so simple. Here was something she could do – a vehicle for prayer. Instead of getting up in the morning and rather sleepily trying to think of something to say to God, here were words which could be used to express her penitence and thanksgiving and worship. Here was a lectionary which steered her through the Scriptures and related to different seasons of the Church year. Here was both a framework and a springboard for her own prayers.

The Daily Office is a simple structure for prayer developed by the early Church from the Jewish synagogue services of Bible readings and psalms. A Daily Office of some kind probably formed some part of the prayer life of Jesus and the disciples. Through Church history the Office has been the backbone of prayer in the Church, particularly in religious communities, with up to seven different services at different times of day. For most Christians leading busy lives one Office a day, either Morning Prayer or Evening Prayer, is sufficient. The Office gives us words to pray and a balanced structure which contains confession, thanksgiving, psalms, set prayers and Scripture. Although some help is needed to begin with, once a person is established in a discipline of praying through the Daily Office, the foundation of prayer can be laid for a lifetime. Through Morning or Evening Prayer and the different readings, a person's own prayer life is linked in with the prayer of the whole Church.

To pray the Daily Office you will need a service book and, usually, a lectionary.[3] As with the first framework, you will need about fifteen minutes rather than five and you will need to spend a few minutes in quiet preparation for prayer.

The first part of the Office is confession, followed (in the mornings) by a psalm of praise. When used regularly, these words become very familiar and comfortable vehicles for prayer. This preparation of confession and praise is followed by slowly reading a psalm, taken from the lectionary. As we saw in chapter six, it is very important somehow to build our own prayer lives around the spirituality of the Psalms – words of prayer and praise used by Jews and Christians for many centuries.

A PRAYER TIME BASED AROUND THE DAILY OFFICE

1 *Preparation:* silent prayer. Sentence from Scripture.

2 *Confession:* using the form in the service.

3 *Praise:* using Psalms 95 or 100 or the Easter Anthems.

4 *Psalms:* following the lectionary.

5 *Bible reading(s):* following the lectionary. Follow this with prayerful reflection on the readings.

6 *A canticle and the creed:* (optional).

7 *The Lord's Prayer and collects.*

8 *Intercession and thanksgiving:* following whatever form you develop.

The Psalms are followed by one or two readings. If you decide to use two readings then one should be taken from the Old Testament and one from the New Testament, following the lectionary. These readings should be approached in the same way you would approach Bible reading when using notes. Read the words slowly and prayerfully and listen to what God is saying to you through them. The readings can be followed by a canticle (a song of praise from Scripture) and the creed – but these two elements should be optional to a person praying on his or her own. A time of prayer then begins with the Lord's prayer and three set prayers (or collects). There should then be time and space for personal intercessions or a longer time of quiet meditation or worship. Other elements of prayer can be included from the prayer book as you find them helpful.

Understanding and using the Lord's Prayer

The Bible contains a great many prayers and helps to prayer (including the whole Book of Psalms). Of all these prayers the greatest and deepest is the prayer that Jesus taught his disciples. It is very important that new Christians are taught what this prayer means and how to begin to pray it and to live it. It is clearly a prayer which Jesus means his people to use each day (since we are to pray for our daily bread). The Prayer itself forms Jesus' answer to the question, 'Lord teach us to pray'. Each line and phrase has many layers of meaning which would make a chapter in themselves. Rightly understood, the Lord's Prayer is a powerful tool for Christian growth and discipleship.

Adding to the basic framework

Once a person has become established in a basic discipline of prayer there are a number of areas which are worth exploring as a way of building on that framework which will allow a friendship with God to deepen and grow through the years. In general, it is best that this development is taken quite slowly – don't try and use all of these ideas at once or the result will be spiritual indigestion not spiritual growth. Think and pray about what is right for you (or a person you are helping) at any particular time.

(a) Practising the presence of God

I once asked a group of new Christians to discuss how they prayed from day to day. People gave various answers. One young woman, in the corner of the room, became very frustrated with all the talk about the difficulty of prayer and different methods. 'Oh', she said 'I just rabbit on to him all day long. Is that all right?' We assured her it was – and that she had been given a great gift which comes easily to some people but others have to work at.

Although it is good to have a set time of prayer most days, it's good also to develop and grow in a sense of the Lord's presence with us each moment of the day. Many Christians have that sense of his presence at the beginning of their Christian lives but quickly lose it in the first six months to a year as the outward form of religion replaces the inner reality of relationship.

In the early part of my ministry as a curate I became frustrated with visiting people in their homes and talking about everything but Christianity. We would discuss mortgages and the weather and the state of the economy – but never the Lord and what he was doing. It was not my habit, in those days, to listen to God – but one night, walking home in a mood of immense frustration, I asked God to show me why my conversation with people never got beyond the superficial. I was expecting, as you might guess, that God would show me it was all their fault. The answer that came back was rather different. 'You can't talk about me because you don't know me' was his answer. Although I was fairly regular in my set prayers I had lost that deep sense of walking with Jesus and coming to know him better as a friend that had once been part of my Christian life.

There are different ways to practise the presence of God. Most of us have to work at it to begin with. Simply remembering he is with us is a glorious truth which can transform most days of our lives and most activities we engage in. Developing a dialogue with the Lord about the things we are doing and the plans we are making is a way of building friendship. Telling him about the events of the day and the difficulties and joys we face builds that sense of intimacy and closeness and also gives us a way of catching his perspective as well as our own. As Christians we have been given the gift of friendship with the creator of heaven and earth. Few of us, I suspect, ever enter into the richness of that friendship. We keep the door of our lives firmly closed. Growing to maturity will often mean doing some building in this area of our lives.

(b) Developing a journal

A second way of growing in that sense of walking with God over the months and years is to begin to write things down. This will not suit everybody – especially if a person has not been used to writing about anything in recent years. If you decide to try to make a journal, it's good to have a special book for that purpose. Begin by writing down the way you became a Christian and the story of your journey with God so far. Make a note of any particular ways he has spoken to you, any Scriptures or signs you have been given, any questions you have about the future and any courses of action you need to take. Most people find that it's not really worthwhile (or possible) to make notes in a journal every day other than at very special times of the year or of their life. Keeping one from time to time, over a period of years, enables you to look back and see trends and patterns in your Christian life and the different places where God has been at work.

(c) Learn some spiritual exercises

When Paul is writing to Timothy he talks about getting into shape spiritually being very like getting into shape physically.[4] If we are out of condition physically or we need be in top condition for a particular event, then we need to take some exercise which normally consists of simple movements repeated regularly. Over time these physical exercises build greater physical fitness.

The same principle applies to getting in good shape spiritually. If we are getting spiritually flabby and out of condition – or if we want to move deeper spiritually – then we need to get in spiritual training. One of the best ways to train is to learn and practise spiritual exercises.

Sometimes these spiritual exercises can be done as part of our basic discipline of prayer for a specific period of time (such as Lent or Advent or before a special mission). Sometimes they need a longer period of time than we can give every day. One possible pattern is to set aside an hour or so a week in certain periods of the year for this kind of spiritual exercise in the same way that many people set aside an hour a week for physical aerobics or fitness training. Here are three spiritual exercises which may be helpful to you.

Meditation on a Bible verse Instead of reading a short passage of the Bible in a fairly superficial way each day take one verse for meditation. Repeat it to yourself over and over again either in your mind or aloud and listen to what God is saying through the different words and phrases. You may be able to focus each day or a week on a different word in the verse. Eventually you will find, if you meditate on a verse, that the particular verse will become an ongoing source of nourishment and refreshment for your spiritual journey.

Imaginative contemplation Take a passage from the gospels and enter into the action with your imagination. As always, take a few moments to be quiet and to seek God's grace as you pray. Read through the particular scene and then imagine yourself in that place. Imagine the sights and sounds, the smells, the weather, the time of day, the clothes, the different textures on your skin and the different emotions as the scene unfolds. Spend time watching what happens in the scene. Think about your own feelings towards the different characters in the drama being unfolded. After the scene is played out, again in your imagination, meet with Jesus and talk with him about what you have witnessed and what that has revealed about your own life. As the prayer comes to an end, collect up the good things you have received and give thanks to God for them. You may like to make a note of anything you have learned or received.[5]

Looking back with thanksgiving This is an exercise to build thankful hearts, a sense of God's presence in our lives and a sense of what is really important. It is best done at the end of a day.[6]

After a moment of quiet preparation and a prayer for God's grace, look back over the past day (or week) and give thanks for all of God's goodness. After you have given thanks for the most obvious things really try and stretch yourself in thanksgiving and appreciation for the less obvious gifts and graces from the Lord. After this period of thanksgiving look back in detail over the day (or week) and ask the question: 'Lord, where have you been in my life today?' Replay each scene or part of the day and ask whether and where God was in each place. The joy of this exercise is that we will often discover that he was there at the moments we least expected as we look back through the lens of thanksgiving. As you finish your look back over the day you may need to say sorry for the places where you sinned or failed him. Then end on a note of thanksgiving and praise.

(d) Learning to listen to God

God is a God who reveals himself and who communicates with his people. Learning to listen to God through the Bible or through prayer takes some perseverance over a number of years. We need to learn to recognize his voice. If we have never heard anything from God, that may be hard at first. To use a very simple illustration, imagine trying to tune in a radio to a station you have never heard before. The first few times you hear it, you may not even recognize what you are receiving. Over the years, as you become familiar with the sound of that particular station, you will be able to tune in much more quickly and with greater confidence.

The Bible tells us that when God speaks he uses a still, small voice. We are more likely to hear him if we are listening regularly. We learn to listen through using the Bible, as outlined above, but also through simply attending to him and waiting on him. The young Samuel's prayer is an excellent one for the young Christian to learn: 'Speak, Lord, for your servant is listening.'[7]

The Lord may speak to us about a number of different issues in our lives to guide us, correct us and encourage us. He may speak to us in a number of different ways, through the Bible, through his creation, through other Christians or as we wait on him in prayer. Each new Christian needs to be equipped with a few simple rules for discerning whether or not it is God who is speaking. We may, after all, simply be listening to our own imagination or to the enemy. Here are some simple tests to apply:

HOW DO WE RECOGNIZE GOD'S VOICE?

1 *Is what you have heard consistent with the Scriptures?* If it is, then it may be from God. If it isn't – then we should discard it.

2 *Does what you have heard lead to an increase of faith, hope or love in yourself or in other people?* Again, if it does, then this may well be God's word to you.

3 *Does what you have heard draw you towards God or away from him?*

4 *If you have a word for someone else is it for their upbuilding, encouragement and consolation?*[8] If it is not, then you have no right to share it.

5 *Is what you have heard consistent with what you believe God has said to you on earlier occasions?*

6 *Are you willing to subject what has been said to the discernment and wisdom of other Christians?*

(e) Developing our prayer for others

Intercession is a vital part of Christian prayer even if it is not the whole part. Some ideas for developing intercession as a tool for building others to maturity are given in Chapter 3. Every new Christian needs to learn how to pray for others with understanding. Most of us do not have very good memories and a useful aid when we pray for others is to have a list of names and situations which we can lift regularly to God in prayer. This list will include our family and close friends, our local church, perhaps those in our home group, those we are praying for who are not yet Christians and certain causes or situations in national or international life as God lays these on our hearts. Many of us are also helped and built up in faith by keeping a list of prayer requests and being able to see how God answers these over time.

(f) Times for spiritual growth

As we grow as Christians, so our prayer life needs to grow and expand and so we will need to take in new resources for prayer from the Bible and from Christian tradition. Most Christians are helped by some time each year set aside to grow in prayer and in our relationship with God either through a quiet day or a residential retreat. The sort of day or retreat we try will need to be thought through carefully. For some people it's a good thing to step outside their own tradition. For others it can be unhelpful, especially at first. However there are a large number of retreat houses and centres for renewal around the country which give opportunities for space and spiritual nourishment in this way.

Finally, the truth that all of us need to go on growing in prayer – and that there are so many different ways to grow – highlights the need for most of us to have someone we can talk to about our spiritual life regularly as we grow in our discipleship. The local church needs to be equipped to offer help and guidance in prayer as part of its ministry. If that help is not available in your own church, then your vicar or pastor may be able to point you to other people outside your own situation who can be of help.

Study Guide

TRACK ONE

For Ministers and Church Leaders

Questions for reflection and discussion

1 Think of half a dozen people in your Church who have been Christians for under two years. How do they pray? How do you expect that they will go on growing in prayer in the next five years?
2 What are the advantages of praying around a framework of the Daily Office as opposed to using Bible reading notes?
3 How many people in your congregation are aware of the possibilities of retreats, quiet days and spiritual direction?

Ideas for sermons and training courses

1 A six-week practical course on 'Learning to Pray'.
2 A sermon series on the Lord's Prayer, line by line.
3 A church quiet day in a local retreat centre with a guest speaker from a different Christian tradition.

TRACK TWO

For Group Leaders

GROWING IN PRAYER

Introductory exercise

Ask the group to break into threes and to discuss their own life of prayer. Stress the need to be honest and encouraging within that threesome. Especially ask people to talk through their normal pattern of daily prayer, whether they pray at all, whether they use Bible reading notes, etc. Ask the small groups to identify any major difficulties in prayer and summarize these with the whole group.

Finding a basic structure for prayer

Use the material from the chapter on misconceptions in prayer and on praying using Bible reading notes and prayer through the Daily Office. You will need to have some samples and examples with you of undated and dated notes and of Office books and lectionaries.

Follow the teaching input with another short session in small groups so people can decide any action they need to take in the light of what you have shared.

Bible study: the Lord's Prayer

Supply each small group with a table containing the lines of the Lord's Prayer in the left-hand column and a blank space in the right-hand column. Ask people to write opposite each line of the prayer what they think it means – in different words.

Go through the Prayer a line at a time in the whole group giving some teaching input as well as sharing the answers already given.

Prayer exercise – building a list for intercession

Supply each member of the group with a sheet of paper on which to make a plan for daily prayer and a list for intercessions. Have a time of silent reflection as people work on their plans and intercession lists individually. Then have a time for sharing the lists in small groups and praying for one another as people seek to go further in prayer.

TRACK THREE

For Those Working One-to-One

Bible study: the prayer life of Jesus

Look at the following passages together and see what you learn about the way Jesus prays: Mark 1:35; Mark 6:46; Luke 4:42; Luke 5:16; Luke 6:12; Luke 11:1–4.

Building a basic framework

Talk through what is happening now in terms of growing in prayer.

Work out a basic framework for a life of prayer and how that should be put into practice.

Adding to the basic framework

This may be something you need to keep returning to over the next few months as appropriate rather than tackle in one session now. Be sensitive to what God is doing.

TRACK FOUR

For Those Working on Their Own

Daily Bible readings

Some of the great prayers of the Old Testament

Mon: *Genesis 18:16–33* Abraham's prayer for Sodom
Tue: *1 Samuel 2* Hannah's song of thanksgiving
Wed: *1 Kings 8:22–53* Solomon's prayer of dedication
Thurs: *Nehemiah 1:1–2:5* Nehemiah's prayers
Fri: *Daniel 9:4–19* Daniel's prayer
Sat: *Psalm 51* A great prayer of confession
Sun: *Psalm 139* A great prayer of openness to God

Longer exercise

Take time to reflect on your own life of prayer in the light of this chapter.
What should be your basic framework of prayer?
How do you need to build on that framework?
Make notes in your journal and, if possible, discuss your decisions with someone else.

NOTES

1 Matthew 6:5–8
2 Undated notes are produced by the main Bible reading agencies
  – several produce particular guides for new Christians.
3 To use the normal Anglican Daily Office you will need a dated

lectionary, a Bible and an ASB. If you can't afford an ASB – or
the person you are advising would be put off by a huge prayer
book – you can buy 'Morning and Evening Prayer' as one
booklet and use your Bible for the Psalms. The Franciscan Office
book is also growing in popularity.

4 1 Timothy 4:8
5 For further help in praying in his way see Gerard Hughes, *God of
Surprises*, Darton, Longman & Todd, 1982.
6 This exercise is based on the 'Awereness Examen' of Ignatius.
7 1 Samuel 3:10
8 1 Corinthians 14:3

eight

Growing in Knowledge

I myself am convinced, my brothers, that you yourselves are full of goodness, complete in knowledge and competent to instruct one another.
Romans 15.14

As we have seen, growth in knowledge is sometimes seen as the only yardstick or measure of Christian maturity. This is a dangerous mistake in a church or individual; there are a number of other key areas of Christian maturity and growth. However, growth in the knowledge of the Christian faith remains vital, particularly in Key Stage 2. What are the different areas in which a new Christian needs to grow in knowledge in the first two to three years of their Christian life? And how is that growth to take place? This chapter examines four main areas where growth is needed. For the first, let's witness an imaginary series of meetings between a vicar (John) and a new member of his congregation (David) taking place over a period of two years.

Knowledge of the Bible

David Thanks for making time to see me, John. I know you have a lot on your plate. One of the home group leaders suggested I come and have a chat.

John It's really good to see you David – what was it you wanted to think through?

David I really feel that I want to get to know the Bible better, but I don't know where to begin. I remember bits of the gospels from school days. I enjoyed the Bible study we did in the Christians for Life group. Most of the time I can follow the sermons in church. But now that I've joined a home group I just feel so ignorant. The others all seem to know the Bible really well – and I haven't got a clue.

John Have you ever tried to read it for yourself?

David I had a go a few months ago – I dug out my old school Bible, opened it at Genesis and had a go. But it was too difficult to understand. I'm not very good at reading books anyway – but I couldn't make head nor tail of most of it. Normally I would have just given up – but something inside me really wants to get to know this book and keep trying – which is why I've come to talk to you.

John Let's have a think then. First you're going to need a new Bible by the sound of it – one in modern English. That cuts out the 'thees' and 'thous' and some of the difficult words. Quite often we give new Bibles to those who've recently become Christians. Would you like one of these?

David Yes please. Would you like me to pay for it?

John No – it's a gift. If later on you want to buy one for another new Christian, then you'd be welcome to. This Bible that we use has a number of helps in it for new Christians: maps and charts and introductions to the different books. Most people find it really helpful.[1]

David Thanks – it looks really good. But where do I start?

John It's not always best to start at the beginning. The Bible is much more like a library shelf than just one book. Most people find it better to start with one of the gospels. At the back of the Bible there is a Bible reading plan which takes you through Mark's gospel first and then gives you, in a year, a tour of every book, with the contents arranged in themes.

David That does look useful, John. I never realized it would be so straightforward.

John Most people don't, David, and they never move on. There are just a couple of other things you may find helpful. The first is you'll come across a few things, even with the reading guide, that you don't understand. There are books you can go to to look them up. Most libraries have them – or you might like to ask for a good Bible handbook for

Christmas.[2] The second thing is that, when you're starting to read the Bible, it's often good to have someone to meet with from time to time so you can ask about anything you don't understand. I can put you in touch with someone in the church if you like.

David How would that work?

John It's very simple really – you just agree to meet every two or three weeks and agree on a reading plan. Then, while you're reading, jot down anything you're not too sure about and you can discuss it when you meet together.

David That sounds excellent. Could you sort that out for me?

John I'll see if we can set that up by the weekend. The last thing is that from time to time there are courses either here or elsewhere in the area to help people get into the Bible a bit more. Keep your eyes on the newsheet for anything that's coming up.

David Thanks John – I'll do that. George was telling me about a correspondence course he's doing from a college – any chance of starting on that?

John You'll probably find you need to walk before you can run, David. Maybe in a year or two that might be useful. For now just concentrate on getting familiar with the different books and what's inside them. Come back to me if you've any problems. Otherwise – why don't we have another chat like this in, say, a year's time?

A year later

John So, David, how's it gone? Are you feeling a bit more confident with the Bible than you were a year ago?

David It's gone really well John, thanks. Despite all my good intentions I'm still only about halfway through the reading plan. There were a couple of gaps in the year when I hardly looked at the Bible. One of the best things has been meeting with Stuart every two or three weeks and having someone to talk to about what I've been reading.

John I know Stuart's really enjoyed it as well – he's never done anything like it before. And how's the group going?

David That's the problem now really. I don't feel as out of my depth as I used to. At least I know which half of the Bible Romans is in – and I've got some idea of the history and the background. But the others in the group seem to get so much more out of a passage than I can. We got together in small groups last week and everyone else in my group had so much to say about just a few verses. I hardly had anything to put in – although I'd spent time reading it before the meeting. Ken, the group leader, has asked me to think about leading a study and I'm petrified.

John I wouldn't say you were quite ready for that yet. But I think it is time for you to change gear a little in your Bible reading. Are you still happy to go on meeting with Stuart?

David Yes – if that's OK with him.

John As far as I know it is. What I want to suggest to you now is that you spend a bit less time just reading the Bible – although you may want to carry on with your study plan – and spend a bit more time thinking about what it means.

David How would that work?

John I'd suggest you take a short book of the Bible – 2 Timothy is a good one to begin with. Each time you meet, agree to look at just one chapter. Try to read the chapter through verse by verse yourself, working out in more detail what it means. I'll ask Stuart to do the same. Then when you meet together, instead of dealing with lots of general questions you can compare notes on the passage. I think that way will help you see how to begin to understand and apply the Bible as well as simply to read it. Perhaps half way through the year then you might have a go at leading a study, if Stuart helps you prepare it.

David 2 Timothy has only got four chapters – where would we go after that?

John When you're reading the Bible in this way don't bother too much about how much ground you're covering. It's going deeper that's important. But after 2 Timothy I would suggest some of the Psalms – and then perhaps have a go at John's gospel. But, in the main, it's for you and Stuart to decide. The other thing you might do while you're reading a particular book is have a look at a simple commentary to get you started. You'll find something on most books in the Christian bookshop.[3]

David Thanks John. That all sounds really good. How long do you suggest we go on like this?

John I would guess another six months to a year is about right, David. But you and Stuart will both know when it's time for something different. Come and see me again when that happens.

Ten months later

David It all worked really well, John. Stuart's helped me really to begin to get inside the Bible and think about what it means as well as to know what it says. I've led two studies in the group now – both a bit amateurish, but the others were really encouraging. As you know, Ken's asked me if I'd consider being a co-leader now. I wanted to know what you think.

John That sounds fine to me, David. You've got a real love for the Bible now and you have some of the tools to begin to share the truth with others.

David I was hoping you'd say that. You know as well that Stuart and I have had to stop meeting together. He's got promotion at work and just doesn't have the time. Things were kind of coming to an end anyway now. I still feel I'm just beginning to get to know the Bible. Is there any other way I can really begin to go deeper?

John Remember that we talked about that correspondence course a couple of years ago – and I said you weren't ready then?

David And I wasn't. . .

John But you may well be now. How about it? It would give you the chance to do some more reading and study. There would be some essays to write. It's a chance to get involved with some of the background issues of the Bible – and to find out where Christians disagree as well as where they agree. . .

David Just like in the home group you mean! Yes, John, it sounds a good idea. Let me pray it over for a few days and read through the literature. But it sounds to me as if that's a good next step. I'm always wanting to go deeper. . .

John There's just one more thing I was going to ask you, David.

David What's that?

John A man called Tom came over to see me last week. He's just recently become a Christian and, like you a couple of years ago, he's no idea where to begin. I gave him a Bible. Is there any chance that you could begin to meet with him regularly – just like Stuart did with you – and begin to answer his questions?

New Christians go through a number of different stages in their relationship with the Bible as described in the dialogue above and the table below.

---

1 *Ignorance:* wanting to find out more – but not knowing where to begin.

---

2 *Learning what it says:* being equipped with a good Bible, some background information, a reading plan and (if possible) someone to ask questions. Reading should focus on content and becoming familiar with the text, listening to sermons and doing group Bible study.

---

3 *Learning what it means:* learning to apply the message of the Bible to a person's own life. Knowing where to receive guidance and help in this from books and from people. Taking part in and leading group Bible study. If possible looking at short passages in some depth with one or two others.

---

4 *More serious study and teaching others:* learning to lead a good group Bible study and to lead others in study. Undertaking a study course of some kind which will deepen and stretch thinking and understanding.

Most people will have reached '1' by the end of an evangelism-nurture group. It is then that further help is needed (just when people are too often left to their own devices). The task of guiding people through '2' and '3' is the task of nurture in

Key Stage 2. The end result, in Paul's words, is not only that people are complete in knowledge but are also competent to instruct one another. Not every Christian will want to go on studying through correspondence courses and the like – but most need to be equipped with the tools to do their own personal Bible study and to be nourished in faith through this means.

Knowledge of Christian teaching

As well as growing in the knowledge of the Bible and the ability to use it, most new Christians will need more detailed instruction in different aspects of Christian doctrine. Only a very limited amount of doctrine can be taught and absorbed through an evangelism-nurture group. Not everything will make sense the first time around. There is a great need to develop more understanding in the key doctrines of the faith as people grow and develop.

One of the most significant and helpful ways of growing in the knowledge of Christian teaching is through the cycle of the Church's year. Every year, in worship, we return to the essentials as we celebrate and remember the birth, ministry, passion, resurrection and ascension of Jesus, the gift of the Spirit, the doctrine of the Trinity and the second coming and last judgement. There is a great need at the major Christian festivals to take people deeper in their understanding of truth and to resist the temptation to remain at the shallow end of the doctrinal pool in sermons and worship.

Generally speaking there are far fewer resources available for helping people to grow in their knowledge of Christian teaching than there are for helping them to study the Bible. Yet this remains a vital area precisely because new Christians will encounter a large number of different teachings on (say) the divinity of Jesus within our very multicultural society.

Developing a Christian mind

Growing in knowledge means more than accumulating a larger number of facts, books or truths about the Christian faith. It also involves developing a Christian mind – being able to think in a Christian way about all kinds of things in daily life. Very often when a person comes to faith we bring with us all kinds of wrong ideas and ways of thinking which are very unChristian. It is these which need to be challenged.

Take a typical group of people in an evangelism-nurture group or a new home group. What kind of ways might they need to grow in developing a Christian mind? Here are three examples:

George has been taught from an early age that men are vastly superior to women, that a woman's place is to stay at home and look after the children, that the man's role in life is to be the breadwinner and that a man is to expect complete obedience from his wife and children. In the early months of his Christian life he finds certain things encourage him in these views in the life of the church. Most of the important jobs in the church are done by men (including all the practical ones and anything to do with money). There are several passages in the Bible which seem to support the idea of the man being in charge and the woman obeying his every command. What's more, there are several other men in the church who clearly think and behave in the same way that George does.

After George has been in the home group for several months, Kev and Julie, the leaders, decide to challenge him gently on the issue – particularly as George's attitude clearly isn't helping his wife, Joan. Their first approach is indirect. One evening of the group's programme is given over to a study of male and female in the Bible: the ways we are different and the ways we are similar. As an introduction to the discussion, Kev and Julie share very honestly how becoming Christians has affected their own marriage and their way of relating to each other. George really respects Kev and is very challenged to hear how much more of a servant Kev has become to his wife and family since he encountered Christ. Kev follows up the meeting with a number of conversations with George on the same subject. Gradually light dawns and George's whole attitude begins to change.

Amanda was brought up in a white home in a white neighbourhood where anyone with a different coloured skin was despised and insulted. When she was converted her racist attitudes remained as a very deep part of her character. This caused no immediate problem (as she attended a predominantly white church) until Amanda was elected to the church council. In the course of a very heated discussion about inter-faith relations in the town Amanda came out with a series of extremely offensive and highly racist remarks. To the vicar's shock and horror these remarks did not disturb most of the PCC in the slightest. Most people seemed to agree.

After some thought and consideration the vicar held a special training session for his church council. He invited along a small number of Christian friends from different ethnic communities to talk about their own experience of Christ within their own culture. He himself gently led the council through a Bible study on God's love for all peoples. During the evening there was a real bond of fellowship and several friendships began between the different communities.

Pauline has recently been ordained and serves in a large suburban church in a wealthy part of the city. One of Pauline's passions as a Christian is ecology and she spent two years working in India before training for ordination. Within the church she discovers, to her horror, there is no concern at all for the environment. People use their cars without thinking; there is a tremendous waste of paper; green issues are regarded as cranky rather than Christian.

Over the three years that she has been part of the church Pauline effects an enormous change first through her example and then through her teaching. Wherever possible she walks or cycles rather than drives. She is careful in her use of resources and wherever possible shares her possessions with those around her. Comments about ecology crop up from time to time in her sermons. She arranges a Tear Craft evening and is able to persuade the church mission committee to give money to enable businesses to start up in developing countries rather than simply relieve poverty. Eventually, with a few others in the church, she is asked to arrange a whole service around the theme of caring for God's world. Through the ministry of one person a whole congregation is learning to think in a more Christian way about a very important issue – a vital part of growing in knowledge.

Knowledge of Church history

The final, important area where people need to grow in knowledge is in their understanding of Christian history in order to develop a sense of perspective on the present day and also to learn the lessons of the past.

A great many Christians in the second half of this century talk (and sometimes write and preach) as though nothing significant had taken place in Christendom from the events described in the closing chapter of Acts until their own conversion (or the beginning of the movement with which they are associated). In fact, as we know, we have now had almost two thousand years of Christian history. There are a great many negative lessons we can learn from every period of that history. But there are a great many positive things we need to hear as well.

A knowledge of the history of the Christian church is unlikely to be supplied by study groups and house groups, which will rightly focus on the biblical material. Apart from, perhaps, some occasional teaching on the saints, it is unlikely to be a good or right subject for sermons in church. Nor are there many books (other than academic ones) which can give new Christians a beginning here. That means there is all the more need for some concentrated teaching on the main outlines of Church history in some non-Sunday setting through a midweek course or mini-conference. It is not likely to be the kind of subject which sets people on fire for Christ or increases their usefulness to the local church (in the short term). It may be difficult (though not impossible) to make the subject appear relevant to present-day Christianity. But in maintaining the overall health of the church over a period of time it is a vital subject to tackle.

Any moving together of Christians from different denominations, in particular, depends on some outline understanding of history: perceiving that what we have in common predates that which divides us. The study of Church history forewarns us against some of the dreadful errors which Christians have made in earlier generations and also enables us to reflect on their strengths which we may have lost sight of in our day. Above all, the more we study Christian history, the more we gain a sense of the vast sweep of God's work in and through the Christian Church in every generation and in many different cultures. The Church in our day, in our locality, is just one manifestation of the whole Church of God. We ourselves are just a small part of God's family seeking to serve him in our generation in the best possible way we can. We need to appreciate and treasure the good things from the past whilst not being afraid to move forward to new things in the future.

Study Guide

TRACK ONE

For Ministers and Church Leaders

Questions for reflection and discussion

1 How are people equipped to read and study the Bible for themselves within your own church? Did you learn anything from the chapter in this area?

2 Make a list of the main Christian doctrines in the creed. By each item make a note of the last time you gave some substantial teaching at Sunday services on this particular theme. Mark the three areas where there has been least teaching. Which one needs to be tackled first?

3 How much Church history do your church members know? How can you help them to learn some in a relevant and exciting way?

Ideas for sermons and training courses

1 A course or mini-conference giving an overview of the Old Testament or the New Testament.
2 A series of sermons on neglected doctrines (see 2 above).
3 A Lent Learning School giving a number of different options for courses and run by several different churches.[4] Courses on the Bible, church history and doctrine can all be included.

TRACK TWO

For Group Leaders

GROWING IN KNOWLEDGE

Introductory exercise

Break into small groups and discuss the following question: Which statement about the Bible do you identify with most?

1 I don't know much about the Bible and I don't really see why I should bother to read it.
2 I really want to get to know the Bible, but I don't know where to begin.
3 I feel I have a good idea of what the Bible is about – but I never seem to get much out of reading it.
4 I know the content of the Bible and I get a lot out of what I read – but I really feel I could go much deeper.

After people have identified with one or other of the statements ask them to change into groups with others who feel the same as they do (all the 1s together, etc). Then ask them to discuss the question: 'What would help us move on?'

Growing in knowledge of the Bible

Spend a few minutes thinking about why it is important – perhaps looking at a few passages. Then either summarize the teaching from the chapter or get two of the group to read the dialogues between John and David, pausing in between each one for questions and discussion.

The aim is to help each member of the group see where they can go from here in their own Bible reading.

Bible study exercises

Ask people to break into groups again (1s to 4s as above). Each group should do something different:

1 One of the co-leaders should lead the 1s (if there are any) through a series of Bible verses which illustrate the importance of God's word and the value of reading it (see Track Four below).
2 One of the co-leaders should take the 2s through a Bible reading plan which has been prepared beforehand. It may also help to have some example Bible reading aids and reference books.
3 The 3s should study a Bible passage together (I suggest Psalm 1 or 2 Timothy 3:10–17). Read the passage and think about what it means individually first and then pool your answers. One of the co-leaders should observe and make one or two comments, but the emphasis should be on people finding out for themselves.
4 Any 4s in the group should be deployed to assist the other groups and helped to grow themselves after the meeting.

Other ways of growing in knowledge

Use some of the other material from the chapter here. What you say will depend in part on the opportunities for Christian learning in your own church and area. You may want to mention a local Christian bookshop, any courses being arranged locally, etc.

If possible, see if any of the group would like to meet with another Christian to read and study the Bible regularly at any of the stages outlined above and see if that can be arranged before the next meeting.

Prayer exercise

Take a few moments to get back into groups again and pray in silence for a while.

Give every member of the group an opportunity to decide

on what is the next move in terms of growing in knowledge. Then ask people to share their resolution briefly and pray for one another.

For Those Working One-to-One

Again, this session focuses on growing in knowledge through Bible reading.

Where are we now?

Take some time to assess where you each are in your Bible reading. If appropriate, introduce your partner to the kind of Bible reading plan outlined above.

Take some time to look ahead over the next week or so's readings and explain anything that might be difficult.

Plan to begin using the scheme in time for your next meeting and carry it forward month by month – assessing where you are going approximately every six months.

A Christian way of thinking

Are there any thoughts or attitudes which need to be worked through here? Is there a particular passage of Scripture which would help?

Prayer together

For Those Working on Their Own

Daily Bible readings: *Psalm 119*

Mon: *Psalm 119:1–24*
Tues: *Psalm 119:25–48*
Wed: *Psalm 119:49–72*
Thurs: *Psalm 119:73–96*
Fri: *Psalm 119:97–120*
Sat: *Psalm 119:121–144*
Sun: *Psalm 119:145–176*

Longer exercise

Work through the chapter with your journal in hand and make notes of areas where you need to grow in knowledge in each of the four areas.

Write down the immediate action you need to take and any help you will need and commit this to the Lord in prayer.

NOTES

1 The most effective and useful Bible to give to new Christians we have found is the *New Life Bible* produced by Bible Society and available in the NIV and GNB translations. It is a very attractive book for adults and young people and the helps and reading plans are excellent. The catch is that it costs about double the price of a cheap hardback edition, but in our experience it's well worth the investment.

2 The Lion *Handbook to the Bible* and the Hodder *Bible Handbook* are both excellent. IVP and Scripture Union have *The Bible User's Manual* which is a good user-friendly introduction and slightly cheaper than the larger handbooks. For those who are not used to handling large books – or those with very little background information – Chris Wright's *User's Guide to the Bible* is first class. All of these books also contain reading plans, as do almost all editions of the *Good News Bible*.

3 The Scripture Union *Lifebuilders* series of Bible studies is an excellent basis for this kind of study. *The Daily Study Bible* can also be extremely helpful. For those who want more material to read, IVP's series *The Bible Speaks Today* is generally very good. The emphasis here should be on commentaries and study guides which are good on application and interpretation as well as content and background.

4 See *Growing New Christians* p. 212 for an example of this.

nine

Growing towards Wholeness

The Spirit of the Lord is upon me, because the Lord has anointed me to preach good news to the poor. He has sent me to bind up the broken-hearted, to proclaim freedom for the captives and release from darkness for the prisoners . . . to comfort all who mourn.[1]

Fiona found herself trapped by agoraphobia by the time she was in her late twenties. She had what most of us would describe as a difficult background and bringing up her children had been a struggle. Now, with most of her life still ahead, Fiona had to rely on invalidity benefit to survive. She was unable to mix socially, continually felt inadequate, lacked the confidence to take up any kind of course or training and found it impossible even to apply for any kind of job.

At the invitation of one of the team, Fiona began helping at the church playgroup. She found it hard to make conversation with the adults but was a great help putting out the toys and playing with the children. After several months she began to open up just a little and talk about her situation. After several more months one of the team members brought her along to church for an evening service and came up with her for anointing for healing. It was a long time before she came to church again – but something happened in that brief encounter with the Lord. When she visited her GP in the weeks following, the doctor himself commented on the change taking place and wanted to know what had caused it as he reduced her medication. Friends in the playgroup team prayed with Fiona and she invited Jesus into her life. Eventually she began attending church regularly. Nine months later she had built up enough confidence to become part of a Christians for Life group and is preparing to be confirmed.

One of the wonderful things about Fiona's story is not that the church has increased its membership by one, but that a person whose life was hard and difficult has been changed and transformed from the inside by the healing love of Christ. As a Church we are called to minister to the poor. Poverty is not only an expression of how much money you have or don't have. Walking around the estates in Ovenden or the markets in Halifax and looking at the faces of the people you can see the mental (and sometimes physical) scars of hard lives. You can sense, if you look, some of the struggle, resignation, hardness, despair and emptiness which grips so many. It is these people that Christ came to set free.

The calling of the Church, as Jesus indicates when he quotes the words from Isaiah 61, is to take the Gospel to the poor, the broken-hearted, the captives and those who mourn.

However, many of the influential models of evangelism which have been developed by the churches in Britain over the last two generations have been developed either in universities (among young people from the most privileged and intelligent groups in society) or in suburbs (among those who have 'succeeded' in life and are comfortably off). When people come to Christ from an affluent suburban or university background they may already be quite well adjusted as people. They are used to learning quickly about new things. They may already have developed, in many areas of their lives, a good self-discipline and self-control. Much of what has been written (and is still being written) about evangelism and nurture from people who have worked predominantly in university or suburban settings pays too little attention to the importance of pastoral care and growing to wholeness in the first years of a person's Christian life. There is a real danger that when courses, models and techniques are transplanted from such a setting into a more ordinary urban environment they fail to take account of this dimension and expect that within a very short time new Christians will be stable, equipped and ready to take on significant ministries.

People who come to Christ later in life from a more ordinary background will need, over time, extensive pastoral care and time for God's love to heal them from within. Growth in both holiness and wholeness will often take years rather than months and calls for patience on the part of those charged with this ministry. One man in our congregation who became a Christian a couple of years ago needed daily contact with one or other member of our staff team for the first six months of his Christian life. Almost two years on he has made great strides, but still needs regular pastoral support, prayer and encouragement.

Even when we are involved with students or those whose outward lives have been more fortunate we should be aware that there are deep areas of their lives where healing and transformation is needed and that this will take time. This chapter looks at the way men and women grow in wholeness in the first years of their Christian life and how we can assist that process. The primary requirements are faith, love, patience and perseverance.

In Revelation 3:20 we are given a picture of a deeper encounter with Christ being like opening a door in our lives and asking him in for a meal. The picture picks up a very common New Testament theme of the presence and the life of Jesus coming to dwell in the life of the Christian. Often I have painted the scene for a new Christian as follows.

Picture your life as being not like a tiny cottage but like a large mansion. There are a great many rooms in the mansion. But because of the way you have lived your life over many years, much of the house is in disrepair. The electricity has been cut off, the drains are clogged up, the roof is leaking and there is dirt, dust and junk in every part of the house. You have heard Jesus knocking on the door of the house and have invited him inside. He comes in – but he comes in not only to eat with you but to begin to work on this broken and derelict house. He comes in with his overalls and toolkit and gets to work.

As you and I would, Jesus begins with the most obvious things that need setting right. The electricity supply is fixed, the roof is mended, two or three rooms are made habitable again, the heating system is repaired. All of that is going on in the first few months of your Christian life. But it doesn't stop there. The Lord's desire is for you to invite him into other sections of the house as well to mend and to repair and to restore. Even the cellars, the attics and the locked secret cupboards can be thrown open to his love and his grace.

Some of this inner healing and restoration will take place without any outside help at all, as Fiona's story shows. As a person spends time in worship and prayer and with the word of God and gets to know other Christians in fellowship and friendship in the first few months and years of his or her walk with Christ, then things will begin to be set right. It just happens. However, in three areas in particular there may be a need for teaching and for prayer either through a course or in an individual setting.

Healing the effects of past hurts

We are all aware that we can be hurt and wounded physically if we fall or are involved in an accident. Often the physical wounds we sustain will heal, provided we receive the correct medical care. Sometimes physical injuries leave us with a permanent disfigurement or disability which we need to learn to live with as best we can.

However, our bodies are not the only part of us which can sustain wounds and injuries. Often, as we go through life, different dimensions of our inner selves (our emotions, our will, our character and our spirit) will be hurt and injured too. When we are injured physically we know that we need medical attention and, in our own country, that attention is always available. However, when we sustain injuries in our inner selves, first, we may not realize the extent of the damage done to us. Second, even if we know that we are hurting and need help, that help may not be available. Consequently we go on our way through life permanently wounded and disabled on the inside. In one dimension or another we live dysfunctional lives. It is not God's will that we should live like this. Once we come to him, he begins to set things right.

Most people, if they are honest, will have sustained some major inner hurts at some point in their life. Psychology reveals that the effects of emotional damage or deprivation from very early years will always persist into adult life. The sorts of hurt that people have sustained in this way include very serious things such as bereavement in childhood or adult life, physical, sexual or emotional abuse, rape, marital infidelity or breakdown, a ruined career, or injury or death to someone we love. Our congregation each Sunday contains people who have suffered from all of these traumas. However it can also include hurts which may not seem so dramatic or obvious but which still deeply affect a person's character years later. These can include rejection (or perceived rejection) by parents; teasing or bullying at school, in the armed forces or similar institutions; being embarrassed by those in authority; early sexual encounters with boyfriends or girlfriends; work relationships; hurt sustained within a marriage; or the divorce of family or close friends.

Past hurts can come to control and dominate lives and lead to serious social, relational and sometimes physical problems. Those who are becoming Christians through churches now, will have sustained these hurts. We need to be prepared to work with God in ministering to them. How can that happen?

(a) Through listening

Listening is a vital activity in pastoral care. All those involved with enquirers and new Christians need to become excellent listeners. It is through listening carefully to people over time that we are able to help them to discern their hurts. It can be especially helpful near the beginning of someone's journey of faith to tell their life story from beginning to end to a Christian friend. Normally this takes more than five minutes over a cup of coffee. Some listening will take place in evangelism-nurture groups and home groups. The most effective listening, however, will happen outside most groups and will take place through the pastoral visiting of those who are new to the faith.

A few weeks ago I made an appointment to see a woman who has recently started coming to church and is new to the Christian faith. I called at about two o'clock and, after initial pleasantries and a cup of coffee, simply sat and listened until about half-past three. The story I heard was a moving and a sad one, mainly about a marriage breakdown which had taken place over a period of years. It was only after listening for eighty minutes or so that I was able to understand her situation. We talked about the Christian faith for about ten minutes before I had to leave – and I was able to link the person in with some others in the church who could take her further. There are, no doubt, some areas of her experience where this lady will need specific prayers for healing. I hope and pray that will happen over the months to come. For the moment, the place to begin was to listen and not to comment.

Churches which are concerned to become effective in nurturing new Christians must have the heart and desire to become listening churches. There is a popular view around that evangelists need to be good at using words and talking. I believe this is a wrong perception. In our own church the best evangelists are the listeners, not the talkers. The desire to listen must extend beyond the clergy to the whole congregation – or at least to all those involved in the pastoral ministry.[2]

(b) Through sensitivity to what God is doing

When someone has shared a hurt from the past with you it may not be right to attempt to pray through that hurt then and there. It may be better to listen some more to what is happening. It may be that there is a healing just in being able to talk about what happened and share it with someone. It may be that you are not the person – or this is not the time or the place – really to pray that one through. Or it may be that the person still has a long way to go in understanding God's love and the way he works in our lives. The person who desires to help other Christians to grow must not only become good at listening to other people. You need to be able to listen to God, to sense his timetable and seek to discern what he is doing within an individual's life. Paul writes to

Timothy: 'Do not be hasty in the laying on of hands.' (1 Timothy 5.22) The verse probably refers to commissioning others for ministry, but it's a useful verse for those called to pastoral ministry as well. Sometimes it's enough – for that time – just to listen.

However, the opposite situation will also arise where there is a need for prayer and no one notices; where a person is beginning to feel acutely the pain of a past hurt and sends out distress signals of different kinds hoping that someone will pick up the signals and come to the rescue. Often, as we have said before, the first few months of a person's Christian life will be a time of great joy. Even if there are inner hurts just below the surface they don't seem to matter just at the moment. Eventually, in God's time, these hurts will begin to surface again and to be a problem and a weight to the new Christian. When they do it is normally a clear sign that this is God's time, now, to deal with this or that situation from the past.

Once a process of inner healing from past hurts does begin, it may continue for several months or even years. Men and women have a great ability to suppress painful memories. In order to heal the wounds inside God causes these memories to surface again, in different ways, which can often be a very difficult experience. Also, one painful memory will be the key to unlocking another a few days or weeks later. In some people it is as though inner hurts from the past are like a series of corks in a bottle – each one keeping down the one below. As God deals with one thing so another is allowed to rise to the surface. In all of this the most basic lesson is not to rush in when we think it's right, but to learn to be sensitive to God's timing.

(c) Through prayer

Not everyone involved in making disciples will be called to the in-depth pastoral ministry of praying through the effects of past hurts. When it becomes clear that a person needs extensive prayer for inner healing, then you may need to refer them on to another Christian with experience of this ministry.

In any church which is growing, this ministry, like the ministry of listening, will need to be growing as well.

Inner healing is essentially a ministry of forgiveness: receiving forgiveness from God for our sins and being able to forgive those who have wronged, hurt or damaged us. Keeping forgiveness at the centre is what makes inner healing such a biblical and Christ-centred ministry. Bitterness and lack of forgiveness are like the poison in the wounds of the past which keep them infected and prevent them from healing over. To pray with someone and allow that poison of bitterness to be released through a decision to forgive is an enormous privilege. In the case of many inner hurts, once the wound has been lanced and the infection of bitterness cleansed, then healing will take place over time.[3] The removal of bitterness allows trust to begin to grow again which in turn allows the person to begin to receive love from God and those around them, which itself brings wholeness.

Many, many times it will be the case that the principal bitterness is against other people who have hurt or damaged the person you are praying with. However, on occasion, a person will have a great deal of bitterness built up against themselves. I have known several people who have been able to accept that God has forgiven them for the failures in the past and for damage done to others, but are unable to forgive themselves for what has happened and continue to punish themselves in different ways. In these situations it is important to talk through the importance of forgiving yourself for what has happened in the past. Often, as with forgiving someone else, it will be helpful to express this in a prayer:

> Lord I thank you that you have forgiven me for . . . I now forgive myself. In Jesus' name, Amen.

Finally, on other occasions, a man or woman may be bitter and unforgiving not against other people or themselves, but against God and may blame God for this or that hurt or disaster in life. When people have suffered very deeply, blaming God is often part of their reaction to the suffering. If the trauma is very recent then the most helpful thing a pastor can do is to listen as people express their feelings of anger or frustration or hurt and to give permission for that to happen. We do not need to defend God or make excuses for him or supply instant solutions or explanations for what has happened. Often, once these feelings of anger have been expressed (as in an argument between a married couple) it clears the air and the person will move on in their understanding of the suffering they have been through. There are many precedents for this kind of anger in the Psalms, in Jeremiah and in the Book of Job.

However, if there are signs that someone is stuck at this point and remains bitter and angry with God over a long period of time, then this does need to be sensitively pointed out and prayed through so that the barrier to receiving God's love can be removed. Again, it can be helpful to lead a person in prayer – after the issue has been talked through. A different form of words is needed. 'Lord, I forgive you. . .' is not a right prayer since the anger and bitterness that is within the person against God is, in the final analysis, irrational (however deeply felt). 'Lord, I let go of my resentment and bitterness against you and Lord I thank you for your love for me' is a better form of words.

(d) Through counselling

In some cases, where the hurt has been deep and the trauma very great, listening and simple prayers for inner healing will not be enough. There will be a need for a new Christian to receive, over time, in-depth counselling over some area of the past or present. For this reason, in any church which is seeking to grow, these Christian counselling ministries do need to develop alongside evangelistic ministries if people are going to come to maturity in their discipleship. Any leaders of a church where these counselling ministries are not available does need to give thought and prayer to the problem over time and, in the short term, find out what resources are available in other churches in the area both for training and for people to receive help.

Being released from irrational beliefs

Each of us has a set of beliefs – not just beliefs about God but beliefs about the way the world is, about people and about life. These beliefs affect our attitudes and our actions – what we do from day to day.

Many of our beliefs are rational – that is they are reasonable and true and help us make sense of the world around us. We set off to catch the bus because we believe it will stick to time. We are kind to our children because we believe this is the best way to bring them up. If you are continually late for work you may get the sack. Rational beliefs affect our behaviour in a good and healthy way: we are making decisions and choices based on the way things really are, not on some false picture of the way the world works.

However, we all have at least some beliefs which are irrational. These are based on wrong ideas we have picked up along the way from influential people in our lives or from our general environment or from the part of life we have experienced. These irrational beliefs can control people's behaviour to a surprising degree. Examples include:

'I must earn happiness'
'Nobody could really love me'
'I can't really trust anyone'
'God has favourites'
'Good things don't last long'
'Whatever I do I should do perfectly'
'My husband/children/friends don't really love me'
'Real men don't show their feelings'

It's not hard to see, from looking at the list, that each of these very common ideas is irrational. It's also not hard to see how any one of them could dominate and control a person's character and affect their relationships, friendships and small and large decisions. These beliefs affect our behaviour in a bad and unhealthy way because we are behaving and making decisions not on the way things are but on the way we imagine them to be.

As with past hurts, we are often helped in being released

from wrong ideas through listening and through prayer. The Lord wants us to live our lives based on reality not unreality. He will be gently challenging and changing our irrational beliefs in many different ways. The process of growing to maturity in this area is one of deliberately putting off what is irrational and putting on the rational. In Colossians Paul describes the importance of putting off the old self and putting on the new.[4] Praying through these wrong ideas can be seen very helpfully as a taking off the old and putting on the new. It is part of the renewing of our mind.

Stages of prayer which you may find helpful in praying by yourself or with others, are as follows:

(a) Identify the irrational belief

You may need the help of friends here – someone to listen to you.

(b) Put off the irrational belief (falsehood)

Like an old, worn-out piece of clothing.

For example: 'In Jesus' name I now put off the irrational belief that crying is a sign of weakness.'

(c) Put on the rational belief (truth)

Put on the new clothing for your mind which God is giving.

For example: 'In your name Lord I put on the truth that crying is not a sign of weakness but a sign of a love and compassion for others and a release for pain and joy. Lord you made me so I can cry sometimes.'

(d) Live it out

It sometimes takes a few days or weeks for the full effect to sink in.

Many people will not just be affected by one or two irrational beliefs but, over time, may well find whole nests of them. For that reason, although it is possible to pray them through with others, it is also desirable that people should be taught how to discern and pray through these wrong ideas themselves as part of their being equipped for the journey.

Receiving God's love

We have seen that one of Paul's key prayers for the new Christians in many of the churches was that they should come to know and comprehend the love of God in a deeper way. Part of growing to wholeness is learning to receive God's love. Many new Christians have a number of barriers in their lives which prevent them from receiving and experiencing his love. Part of caring for people in the first years of their Christian lives and building them up in the faith is helping them to recognize these barriers in themselves and, if possible, overcoming them. The three principal barriers are:

(a) Past sin

As was mentioned in Chapter 4, new Christians will often be helped by making a formal confession. Even if that does happen however, people may find it very difficult to believe that they are forgiven by God – particularly if the sins which are on their conscience are serious and significant ones. The key to helping people is again listening carefully to what lies below the surface and, if the problem is one of past sin, giving clear, one-to-one teaching on the cross and the meaning of the cross and on the wonderful truth that we are put right with God not on the basis of what we have done, but on the basis of what God has done in Christ.

(b) Wrong ideas of God

For many people these are important. Not everyone has a good experience of their own father being kind, gracious and compassionate. Not everyone even knows who their father is. To call God 'Father' may therefore not be helpful to at least some new Christians initially. Others have been brought up with a picture of a God, from their earliest years, who is stern and unforgiving; who is quick to anger and to punish and slow to forgive, to affirm and to love. God is much more like a stern headteacher or authority figure than someone who loves them. Again, the remedy for wrong ideas is the truth as revealed in Scripture. A person whose Christian life is dominated by these kinds of wrong pictures of God needs to be taken to passages in the Bible which describe God's love and compassion and forgiveness.[5]

(c) It is hard to receive love anyway

Some people find it hard to receive God's love because they simply find it hard to receive anybody's love: it is hard to believe that family, friends, parents or anybody else loves them dearly. Often this will be because of the kind of love they have experienced themselves, especially in childhood. Sadly not all children are loved or affirmed by their parent(s). Often the parent(s) have known very little love in their own lives and have been given no model for loving their children. In order to help people here it is important to give clear teaching about the love of God. It is also important to talk through childhood experiences and hurts from the past. But it is perhaps most vital to demonstrate that love in the present within the body of the church: 'No one has ever seen God, but if we love one another, God lives in us and his love is made complete in us.' Christian pastoral care can never be a clinical, dispassionate ministry and can never be reduced to techniques or instant solutions. At its simplest and at its most demanding it is about loving God's people.

Equipping the Church to enable people to grow in wholeness

According to Ephesians 4, one of the ministries needed in the Church to equip God's people for works of service and to build maturity is the pastoral ministry. One of the aims of the pastoral ministry is to enable people to grow in wholeness. For that to take place, I believe that the local church needs to be equipping people for ministry and service at four different levels:

Level 1: a basic ministry of listening

This needs to run right through the different ministries of the church: clergy, home group leaders, lay pastors, leaders of groups for the elderly, parents and toddlers, etc. need to be equipped with basic listening skills. Some kind of listening course should be at the foundation of whatever training is available in the local church for lay ministry.

Level 2: pastoral visiting

Pastoral visiting should not be simply about keeping in touch with people, passing the time of day or following them up when they don't attend church. It should be about meeting with people in their own homes and giving them space to talk about what concerns them. It is in this way that opportunities for growth and ministry will come to light. Pastoral ministry is not a particularly complex ministry; there will be people in almost every church who can be trained and commissioned for the task.

Level 3: prayer for inner healing

A significant number of people in the local church also need to be equipped to pray for people for inner healing in the areas of the healing of past hurts and freedom from irrational beliefs. In any church of more than sixty adults where people are becoming Christians regularly, this ministry needs to be shared by more people than the single minister. Again, like the listening skills, not a great deal of training or expertise is needed: simply the knowledge of a few basic principles and a willingness to learn from and listen to the Holy Spirit combined with the common sense to know when more specialized help is required.[6]

Level 4: pastoral counselling

If these listening and inner healing ministries are operating effectively in the local church it will be only a small number of people who then need to be referred on for in-depth pastoral counselling taking place over a number of weeks or months. Yet this ministry certainly will be needed for some people. In most situations it is preferable that this in-depth pastoral counselling is not given by the senior minister. If it is, then a large proportion of his/her time will be taken up with a very small number of needy people to the detriment of the whole church. It is better that lay counselling ministries are developed over time either within one church or a group of churches. It is important to recognize that training and preparation for this ministry will need to be over a long period of time and almost certainly from outside the local church.[7]

Study Guide

TRACK ONE

For Ministers and Church Leaders

Questions for reflection and discussion

1 Share together your own experience of growing towards wholeness. What elements in the chapter particularly struck you?

2 Are the pastoral ministries described at the end of the chapter developing in your own situation? How are you to make progress in developing these ministries?

Ideas for sermons and training courses

1 A Christian Listeners taster day run by the Acorn Healing Trust.

2 A mini-conference on the basic principles of inner healing.

3 A teaching series for home groups on barriers to wholeness.[8]

4 A sermon series on forgiveness (of others and ourselves) and on releasing our bitterness against God.

For further reading

Listening to Others, Joyce Huggett, Hodder and Stoughton, 1988.
Set My People Free, Mary Pytches, Hodder and Stoughton, 1987.
How Can I Forgive?, Vera Sinton, Lion, 1990.

TRACK TWO

For Group Leaders

Please note that there is enough material in the chapter to cover several sessions – don't try to cram too much into one meeting.

GROWING TOWARDS WHOLENESS

Testimony

If you can, begin the meeting with a testimony from someone who has some personal experience of God working in his or her life in some way through inner healing. Members of the group may like to ask questions afterwards. Follow the testimony with a brief introduction to God's desire for us to be whole people.

Introductory exercise

The leaders will need to have poster/collage materials available. Make a poster or collage of your life. Show the different parts of your life which God has already sorted out. If you can, show the areas where there is still sorting out, healing and growing to be done. Explain your collage to the whole group or a buzz group after you have made it.

The healing of past hurts

Teaching on what inner healing is and how past hurts can affect us in the present. Explore the need to forgive other people and ourselves and to let go of resentment against God. Leave a space for small group response and questions.

Bible study: Jesus' teaching on forgiveness. *Matthew 18:21–35*

Irrational beliefs

Follow the Bible study with a question and answer plenary session in which you give some teaching on irrational beliefs, if time allows.

Prayer exercise

A time of prayer for one another in small groups especially focusing on forgiveness and letting go of bitterness *or* the meditation on Revelation 3:20 from the first part of the chapter.

For Those Working One-to-One

If you have not already done so, listen to each other's life stories over the next two sessions together. Each of you may like to take up to an hour simply to tell the story of your life to the other.

Do a Bible study on Psalm 103 together and talk about any wrong ideas about God.

Explore any areas where unforgiveness or irrational beliefs are a barrier to growth or where any outside help is needed.

Note: Take care that this session does not turn your teaching/pastoring relationship into a counselling one. If any deeper counselling is needed you should normally refer the person on to someone else in the church for this ministry.

For Those Working on Their Own

Daily Bible readings

Mon: *Luke 4:14–28* Jesus' manifesto from Isaiah
Tue: *Luke 5:18–26* Inner and outer healing
Wed: *Luke 6:17–22* Jesus' love for the poor
Thurs: *Luke 6:27–36* Jesus' teaching on love and mercy
Fri: *Luke 6:46–49* Building on the solid foundation of truth
Sat: *Matthew 18:21–35* On forgiveness
Sun: *Luke 10:38–42* On anxiety and priorities

Longer exercise

Inner hurts and irrational beliefs.

Take some time to be quiet and still before the Lord. Read through Psalm 139 and spend some moments reflecting on God's intimate knowledge of you.

With pencil in hand, ask God to show you any areas in your own life where you need to forgive others or yourself or to let go of resentment against God. If you can, pray these areas through now. If there are problems and difficulties, resolve to go and talk them through with someone.

Either now or at a later stage ask God to identify in you any irrational beliefs which affect your faith and life. Pray them through as outlined above.

NOTES

1 Isaiah 61:1–3
2 St George's has benefited enormously through training and involvement with the Christian Listeners programme run through Acorn Healing Trust which teaches people at different levels the skill of listening.
3 For some guidelines on helping people to forgive others through prayer see *Growing New Christians*, pp. 198–9.
4 Colossians 3:1–14
5 Psalm 103 would be a good place to start.
6 I don't know of a good basic course on inner healing which can be easily adapted to the local church's training needs. As in many other areas of equipping for ministry there is a gap in the market between the very basic and the very specialized. In the work on inner healing we have done at St George's we have relied on compiling training courses from a number of different books and sources.
7 St John's College, Nottingham run an excellent series of extension courses in pastoral counselling from a basic six-month introduction to a diploma accredited by Nottingham University.
8 At St George's we made a helpful adaptation of a Vineyard course for one of our home groups to give people a basic understanding of inner hurts and irrational beliefs. Some of the teaching material in this chapter is based on the course, which we called *Break Free with Jesus*. The original Vineyard course on cassette is

entitled *Free to Be* and is available from Vineyard Ministries International. The photocopied handouts for our own course are available from St George's House, Lee Mount, Halifax, HX3 5BT.

ten

Growing in Holiness

God's people are called to be holy as God himself is holy. A key part of growing in Christian maturity and discipleship must therefore be growing in holiness in thoughts, words and actions. Growing holiness as a Christian is not about keeping a set of rules more effectively but about God changing us from the inside out and about us becoming more like Christ through the work of the Spirit in our lives. There is, I hope, something about growing in holiness in every chapter of the book but especially the first, second and fourth. The purpose of this chapter is to take a closer look at the most important stages a new Christian will move through in the first two to three years of their Christian life. Each section is accompanied by a diary entry written by an imaginary new Christian.

(1) Initial change

As was mentioned above, becoming a Christian will often mean a significant change for an adult, certainly in the area of their conscience. What has been dead and sleeping for so long now comes to life, sometimes in a disturbing way. Things which seemed OK to do or say or think are now being challenged from within. Areas which have been neglected for a long time in our lives (such as family relationships or honesty) begin to raise their heads.

It may also be the case that certain areas of life which have been a problem just change. God seems to give grace in different areas to different people. One person may automatically stop swearing. Another may be able to give up smoking. Another will cease to be troubled by sexual temptation, for a time. It is a wonderful sign of God's love and his reality that these changes occur. But they are just a beginning.

Brenda's diary:
Lord, thank you that you've come into my life. Thank you that whole new areas of life have opened up to me – it's like I've been looking at life on a black and white TV for so long and now it's in colour. Thank you for the joy I've got inside. Thank you for the new friends. Thank you for just being there Lord.

And thank you, Lord, for helping me stop swearing. My mouth's been filthy for years – especially at work. I'd just stopped noticing the kind of language I've been using – especially at work. Now all the girls have noticed that I've stopped swearing and they're giving me a hard time. That Rita Johnson's a real . . . well, I won't use the word but you know what I mean. But this is even funnier – their bad language makes me feel all sick inside – especially because I used to talk like that. Anyway, that's enough for now. The vicar said it would help to get some of this down on paper and I suppose that in a way it has. I'll write again soon. . .

(2) Understanding God's ways

Most new adult Christians need to learn God's standards for human life. They haven't learned them before they come to faith and are not automatically given the knowledge on conversion. So it takes time to learn, understand and begin to apply the importance of honesty and truthfulness, the importance of rest in the rhythm of work, and the right ethical standards in sex and in business. New Christians do not come into the church ready laundered. Often, in our own church, new Christians can cause some raised eyebrows among the existing congregation with their language, behaviour or actions. Sometimes the 'elder brothers' forget that the new members of the family have not yet been shown the Father's ways and actually don't know any better.

Hence the importance of teaching new Christians God's

standards for different areas of life as early as possible in their Christian lives. An obvious base for this teaching are the Ten Commandments which set boundaries and general guidelines for our behaviour. These need to be linked with the Beatitudes and other New Testament passages which make it clear that holiness is something we keep aiming for – not something we achieve by keeping a few rules. The teaching will be needed in groups but also needs to be happening from the pulpit. God's grace cannot be understood and appreciated without some understanding of his law. Martin Luther, at one point in his preaching ministry, felt obliged to preach the law before his people could come to understand the Gospel. A modern, secular congregation is in largely the same position.

Brenda's diary:

That was a killer of a sermon yesterday. Really got to me. Nobody had ever told me that Sunday was special. How was I supposed to know? I've right enjoyed shopping on Sundays since Sainsbury's opened. It's more kind of leisurely. He's always stuck in front of the telly on a Sunday afternoon anyway. It's a proper break to get away from the kids and go round the shops. Then that Joe Smith (who, as you know Lord, is my fellowship group leader) tells me that I shouldn't go shopping on Sundays now I'm a Christian. I nearly gave him a right mouthful. It's a good job I didn't really 'cos the vicar said the same thing (only in a nicer way) this morning at church. Said we should respect the Sabbath and keep it holy. That it's your special day and a day we should rest. And that we should be different from the people around us. He said we could decide for ourselves though. So I've decided that pushing a trolley round Sainsbury's is my way of resting on a Sunday afternoon. You can't say fairer than that, Lord. . .

(3) Righting wrongs

As a new Christian learns God's ways there should then come a period of setting right things that are wrong in lives and in lifestyle. The confession of past sin and seeking forgiveness has been dealt with in Chapter 4. I am referring here to things which are still part of the life of the new Christian. Generally speaking, these are not wrongs which will be set right in the first few months of a person's Christian life. It will take some time. In particular, people may need help in the following areas:

(a) Debt and money management

A significant number of people become Christians having incurred heavy debts which they are finding difficult to repay. The fact that they are in debt will (understandably) not be revealed if people can avoid it. There is a sense of shame involved and of not wanting to lose the good opinion of others in the church. For this reason there may sometimes be a case for asking gently about money and an individual's financial position at some fairly early point in their Christian life. Otherwise, the only time people will mention their debts and financial insecurity is when things have reached crisis point.

As with most things, once the problem has been shared and talked through, much practical help can be given. Most new Christians do not need much to convince them that it is better to pay off existing debts as soon as possible and to curb spending until all creditors have been dealt with. The Citizens' Advice Bureau give excellent advice to those caught in financial difficulty. The local church can support with encouragement and prayer. Very occasionally it may be appropriate to give a small amount of emergency financial aid. However, I would always be very cautious in giving such aid if a person is a very new Christian (that is, has been part of the church for less than a year). I have also become cautious about giving such aid in the form of a loan. If repayments do become difficult, this can create an additional pastoral problem in the future. Normally speaking a person needs to be encouraged to take on responsibility for financial debts after they have come to faith as well as beforehand. It is surprising how often things come right, over time, once the matter has been committed to God in prayer.

(b) Honesty at work

For many people, cheating at work in some form or another is accepted practice. This kind of cheating may include taking unauthorized time off and ringing in sick, pilfering from an employer (because everyone does it), filling in dishonest tax returns, overcharging clients for work which hasn't been done and so on.

Pursuing holiness means that if a person has been involved in these practices before becoming a Christian, they do need to be set to rights. Again, it is unlikely that a new Christian will always volunteer information unless the subject is given a chance to come up. Generally speaking, if what is happening involves just an individual, then sorting the problem out is fairly straightforward. The person who is a new Christian simply needs to make a decision to give up the profits of dishonest gain and to stick to the rules – even if no one else is willing to do so. However, if what is happening is a group practice and the new Christian's conduct affects other people as well then the matter will be a good deal more complicated. If a group of employees have been over-claiming a productivity bonus for several years and one of the group, shortly after becoming a Christian, refuses to join in the conspiracy then this is likely to provoke a reaction from other members of the group. The right course of action will be obvious, but the way through the situation will need to be talked through and prayed through before any hasty action is taken, and much support will be needed.

Brenda's diary:

Lord, if you don't mind me saying so, this being a Christian business is getting a bit serious. I'm sorted out on Sundays now by the way. And yes, I did send that catalogue back so I can't buy anything else on the never-never until that debt is paid off. Well, nothing for me anyway. I've got to keep the kids in clothes. But last night was really heavy. What was I supposed to do? It's nearly Christmas and money's short for all the girls – not just me. So they decided to do what we've done before: nick some of the product, sell it through Rita's feller's car boot sale and split the money. All the girls in our section are in on it, including the supervisor. I know it's not right but they threatened to clobber me if I let on. I didn't sleep at all last night when I got home. I'm frightened of what will happen if I do. I'm scared to tell anyone at church. Just show me, will you, what the right path is?

Maybe there is someone I can talk to about it after all. Jackie from Christians for Life works in a job like mine. Perhaps she can help. Thanks, Lord.

(c) Sex

Growing in holiness means more than what is contained in this section of the chapter, but it certainly includes sorting out the sexual side of our lives. The recent comprehensive survey *Sexual Behaviour in Britain* demonstrates that most young people and adults in Britain do not live according to orthodox Christian standards in this area of their lives.[1] Whilst most people outside the churches still pay lip service to ideals of honesty, integrity and truthfulness in the area of sex there is a wide discrepancy between what those outside the Christian community believe to be right and what those inside it believe. For this reason new adult Christians are likely to need more help in coming to terms with their faith in this area of their lives than in any other. I suspect that in most churches this is actually the place where least personal help and guidance is given. Growing in the Christian faith here will mean different things for different people, depending on circumstances.

For the person who is 'happily married' it may mean very little on the surface. However there may be some darker areas of involvement with pornography, fantasies or fetishes to be worked through. It may be that previous sexual relationships outside of or before marriage surface as problems in the present and need to be prayed through. It may be that a sexual relationship within a marriage which has been stagnant or non-existent begins to flourish again. It may be that the sexual relationship within the marriage has become locked into patterns which are unhealthy or in which one partner uses or exploits the other. These, too, may need to be talked through with great sensitivity and confidentiality, particularly if only one partner is a Christian. Not everyone can handle hearing about problems or offering help in this area. Ideally, married people need to know that there is at least one person of each gender in the life of the church with whom they can talk about sex without embarrassment and in complete confidence.

In dealing with new Christians who are married there is a particular need to emphasize the importance of faithfulness within marriage. Sadly, the temptation to adultery seems to be a significantly strong one in the years following conversion. This is partly because of the society around us. In the survey referred to above, 4.5 per cent of married men of all ages claimed to have had two or more sexual partners in the last year.[2] That means that, in British society as a whole, one in twenty men have been unfaithful to their wives in the past year alone (the same figure for women is 1.9 per cent or one in fifty).

The years following a conversion to Christianity by one or both partners in a marriage inevitably involve a period of adjustment for the marriage relationship. For the first time in recent years, close friendships may be formed outside the marriage with members of the opposite sex. In certain churches, these close relationships may involve a significant degree of physical contact as an expression of 'fellowship', which again may be a new experience (and a difficult one). Possibilities exist to form close friendships between the opposite sexes outside marriage or to form close friendships between married couples as people spend time together in small groups. Significant friendships may form between those involved in pastoral and counselling relationships, especially if those doing the counselling have not been prepared to recognize the dangers.

When all of these new opportunities combine with a general freeing up of a person's character, spiritual life and emotions because of the good things God is doing, there is for a time a significant opportunity for the devil to make great mischief and misery through temptation to adultery. Church leaders need to be continually aware of the danger of, for example, pastoral relationships developing into something else, of married couples developing exclusive friendships which turn into adulterous affairs and of platonic friendships (so-called) which develop into affairs. Many, many churches (including our own) can witness to the sadness and devastation to the people concerned and to the whole body which is caused when one of these situations develops into adultery. Part of watching over the flock of God which is in our care[3] must mean being aware of these dangers; creating a climate in the church where other people are aware of them, too, and where it is hard for such things to flourish; and being willing to speak honestly, openly and personally to people at an early stage to warn them against what is taking place.

For the single person Most single people who become Christians as adults have already taken their sexual standards from the world around them. For some (although not the majority) that means a fairly casual attitude to sex; sometimes a multiplicity of partners and limited taboos.[4] For the single person who becomes a Christian this can mean a change from sexual freedom to celibacy outside marriage, which is the biblical standard. Whilst this change comes as a relief to some, many find that this is not easy to achieve. Much help will be needed and this help needs to be given in the context of a relationship where the new single Christian can fail and know that they will be forgiven and welcomed back both by God and by their Christian friends. Walking the fine line between not compromising biblical standards of morality, yet extending love and patience to the person who is trying to work things out in their own life, is not easy.

For the homosexual or lesbian Those who have lived a homosexual or lesbian lifestyle will need particular care and patience to find acceptance and new patterns of life now that they are Christians.[5] They may feel within themselves a sense of shame before other Christians in admitting to aspects of a past lifestyle or a present orientation. They will almost certainly meet homophobia (an irrational fear of homosexuals) in one form or another in the church of which they are part. That will be combined with a misunderstanding of their orientation or condition and (sometimes) misguided attempts to pray for healing.

The people I have encountered in our own congregation who have admitted to an attraction to people of the same sex have done so in the expectation that they will be condemned as people and dismissed from the church. As I understand the Scriptures and the Christian tradition, the person of homosexual orientation is called, like the single person, to live a sexually celibate life once they have come to Christ. As for the single but sexually active heterosexual, there is certain to be a period of adjustment and working through the issues before a settled position is reached.

Those who have lived a homosexual or lesbian lifestyle will need particular care and patience to find acceptance and new patterns of life now that they are Christians. It may help them to be introduced to specialist groups which can help them to work through their sexuality in a Christian context. In some parts of the country such groups will be very accessible, in others very remote. The situation of homosexual Christians is certain to be complicated by the debate about homosexuality and Christianity which is taking place at the moment in most of the major denominations and which is likely to become more important over the next five to ten years. In the course of that debate, the homosexual Christian will hear conflicting voices, some urging an acceptance of homosexual expression as right and normal within the Christian Church and others wanting to maintain the New Testament position, but perhaps not always speaking with love and charity towards those with difficulties in this area.

It is possible for a church completely to ignore the possibility that any Christian will have problems with their sexuality and effectively to sweep the problem under the carpet. To do so shows a lack of compassion and is certain to alienate a small but significant group in the community who have real spiritual needs. As in other areas of the Christian life, clear teaching is needed combined with great pastoral sensitivity.

For the people who are living together but not married A situation which we meet frequently in our own congregation is that of the woman who becomes a Christian and is living in a fairly stable relationship with a partner who is not her husband. Often the couple will have one or more children. What should we advise there?

Generally speaking the issue is not one which we raise directly with people at all in the first few years of their Christian lives. People living in that situation are present when clear Christian teaching is given about marriage. Such people are aware that they can come and talk through their position at any time. Churches will differ on this but here we place no bar on people who are living together in a stable relationship coming to be baptized and/or confirmed or to receive Holy Communion. Where both partners have become Christians we would normally give every encouragement to the couple to review their present situation before God and proceed to marriage in due course. If there are any things that stand in the way of the couple getting married (such as the cost) it may be possible for others in the church to help by contributing in practical ways to the wedding day.

However, where only one partner has become a Christian the situation is more difficult. Often the Christian partner will want to be married, but the non-Christian partner will not want to. Should the Christian partner abandon that relationship (which may involve a very real disruption to the children) if there is no promise of marriage? Or should she or he remain in the hope that eventually the arrangement will be put right before God? I have no doubt that the latter is usually right. During the first two to three years of a person's Christian life this needs to be thought and talked through with those in leadership. Each person needs to be encouraged to discern God's will for him or herself in these areas after thinking through the relevant Scriptures. The Christian partner should be encouraged to live as though married to the non-Christian partner (that is faithfully and with intention of a lifelong relationship).

The church leadership will also need to talk through the extent to which a person in this situation is able to exercise a ministry in the life of the church. Again, this will vary from community to community. In our own church the general practice has been to encourage people in this situation to exercise a ministry as best they can and according to their gifts but that this should not include any positions of leadership or evangelism.

Brenda's diary:

Joe and Martha tackled me tonight, Lord, about not being married to Bert. I must admit I was beginning to dread the subject coming up, especially since we did that study on Corinthians last week. When we talked about Christian marriage I felt myself go red. It wasn't as though anybody said anything or as if anybody would. I think it was just that I knew it was something I needed to talk through. I guess Joe and Martha did, too; in fact I was surprised no one had a word with me about it sooner. I think if they hadn't raised the subject, I would have found it very hard to go back to the group again this week.

Anyway, they were great about it. I explained that Bert and I have been together for ten years. We did plan to get married once, but we couldn't afford it at the time. Then the kids arrived and it just got put off. We've been happy together as well. We have our moments, but I expect everybody does. I said I've never felt that you minded us not being married and they could see the sense of that. It was good to get everything out in the open. They explained that there may be one or two things at church it might not be right for me to do, and I could see the sense of that. But they've got me involved in helping with the old folks now, which is more up my street anyway. We had a really good prayer time afterwards. I really felt you were there, Lord. Martha prayed that I would really know the right time to mention the subject of marriage to Bert. I know I want to get married. I'm just not sure about him. I don't know if the right time will be in the next few weeks or the new few months. I'll just rely on you to show me, Lord. Thanks for understanding, and thanks for Joe and Martha.

(d) Family feuds

There are feuds and divisions in many families. Parents fall out with children and children with parents. Brothers and sisters separate. Quarrels begin and are perpetuated from year to year until the original reason has long been forgotten. Part of God righting wrongs in the lives of new Christians will be the healing and mending of some of these feuds. Again, I have learned to look for this to happen over years rather than in the first weeks and months of a person's Christian life. Almost always the initiative and the timing is God's. For the first months of Christian experience the person seems to be able to live quite happily with the knowledge that they have not spoken to their brother for seven years. Then, in his time, God begins to place his finger on the relationship and tell the new Christian very clearly that a move needs to be made. The first stage of this may mean praying through what has happened and being able to forgive where forgiveness is needed.[6] However, a second stage may involve making the first move to mend and heal broken relationships (and, possibly) asking for forgiveness as well.

This is the point at which the new Christian will need support and help. In my experience, where one member of the family makes a move to end a family feud and, perhaps, apologizes or goes to visit, the move is usually welcomed. However, sometimes, sadly, it isn't. Other members of the family reject the olive branch and the new Christian suffers a worse rejection than before and, sometimes, their faith is knocked because of that. Ministers or group leaders need to be on hand to support, pray and advise.

(4) Growing towards God

After the three stages of first changes, understanding God's way and righting wrongs, the new Christian joins the rest of us in growing towards God gradually throughout our lives. Holiness in this instance is never something we achieve, but is something we are growing in until we are with God.

New Christians, like the rest of us, need to learn to recognize God's hand in our lives in this area. For most people, there is a sense of a cycle. We are going along quite nicely in our Christian lives, aware that we are sinners but unaware of any need to change. God shines his light a little deeper into us and makes us aware of an area of sin. This may be in our actions (how we treat our children), it may be in our words (our tendency to gossip), it may be in our thoughts (dreaming all day long about a new house) or our deep-seated attitudes (we become aware of our ambition). God may shine his light through his word, as we read it or hear it expounded. He may shine it through a series of conversations or relationships or some new situation.

In whatever way the light comes, God allows us to see a little more of our own sinfulness. He rarely allows us to see the full extent of it lest we become discouraged and give up altogether. At that point we repent and come to him in a new and deeper way, asking for grace to change in this or that area of our lives and thanking him, once again, for his grace shown through Jesus. What we have been shown about ourselves in just one area of our lives serves to increase our love for God in every area. Our Christian life continues again, hopefully with a deeper sense of being poor in spirit and relying on God's grace.

For many Christians that cycle of growing in holiness continues at their pace (and the Lord's) year by year. However, many older Christians are helped by the cycle of the Church's year and, at some point, it can be helpful to introduce new Christians into this aspect of the Church's life. The seasons of Lent and Advent in particular are meant to be times of self-examination and of inviting God to shine his light more deeply into our lives to draw up to repentance and faith. In Lent we examine ourselves in order to bring that sin to the cross in repentance and to celebrate Easter with joy. In Advent we examine our lives knowing that one day we will give an account of them to our creator, and as we prepare to celebrate Christmas. The church's year can be a powerful tool as, year by year, we seek to grow in holiness along with the whole of Christ's church.

Study Guide

TRACK ONE

For Ministers and Church Leaders

Questions for reflection and discussion

1 Are there areas of advice in this chapter where you would want to disagree strongly with what is said? What would your own church policy be?
2 What factors in the life of your church challenge people to a deeper holiness?

Ideas for sermons and training courses

1 A sermon series on the way we grow nearer to God.
2 One-off events or courses on the material on 'Righting wrongs'.
3 A weekend conference for singles on sexual ethics.

TRACK TWO

For Group Leaders

GROWING IN HOLINESS

Sharing together

What changes have you noticed in your own life and conduct since you became a Christian? Ask people to discuss in small groups and then pool your answers.

Group exercise

Invent some 'case studies' based on the kinds of situations in the 'Righting wrongs' section. Ask each small group to think for a few minutes about how to advise and help someone in that kind of situation and then ask each group to present their material to everyone else for discussion.

A call to be holy

Much of the teaching in this session should come out of the case studies outlined above. Discuss God's call to be holy and the way he works from within to change and transform our lives.

Prayer exercise

A time of prayer for one another and, if appropriate, a time of open confession.

TRACK THREE

For Those Working One-to-One

You will need to be very sensitive here according to the person you are dealing with. Give some opportunity at least for the more difficult subjects to come up in conversation.

For your Bible study focus on Ephesians 5:1–21.

TRACK FOUR

For Those Working on Their Own

Daily Bible readings

Mon: *Leviticus 19:1–19*
Tue: *Isaiah 6:1–6*
Wed: *Psalm 51*
Thurs: *Luke 4:1–12*
Fri: *Colossians 3:1–17*
Sat: *Philippians 3:12–21*
Sun: *Ephesians 5:1–21*

Longer exercise

An examination of your own life, paying particular attention to:

(a) Major areas where change is needed
(b) The little things where God's call is to be more like Jesus

NOTES

1 *Sexual Behaviour in Britain*, Kay Wellings, Julia Field, Anne M. Johnson and Jane Wadsworth, Penguin, 1994. The survey is the most comprehensive ever on sexual practices in Britain and is based on personal interviews with over 18,000 individuals.
2 Op. cit., p. 203.
3 1 Peter 5:1–4
4 According to *Sexual Behaviour in Britain*, 28 per cent of single men and 17 per cent of single women report two or more heterosexual partners in the last year. Contrary to popular myth, a relatively small proportion of the population have a very high number of sexual partners (5 per cent of men and 0.7 per cent of women report more than ten partners in the last five years); op. cit. pp. 95–6, 103.
5 Until recently, it has been hard to estimate the numbers of people who feel an attraction towards others of the same sex or who engage in homosexual practice. However, in the survey quoted above, 1 per cent of men and 0.5 per cent of women reported that they were 'mostly attracted' or 'only attracted' to members of the same sex. The same proportion of respondents indicated that their sexual experience was mostly or only homosexual (1 per cent of men and 0.3 per cent of women), op. cit., p. 183.
6 See Chapter 9 and *Growing New Christians*, p. 198.

eleven

Faith in the Family – Faith at Work

Faith in the family

Tony is midway through leading a course on discipleship for those who have become Christians in the last eighteen months. There are just eight people in the group. The basic aim of the group is to give teaching and practical help to people in Key Stage 2 of their Christian lives. Tony himself has been a Christian for about five years. He's single and in his early thirties and this is the first group of this kind he's had the chance to lead. The group know each other well. Most became Christians at about the same time, partly through an evangelism-nurture group led by the vicar. The group are mixed in terms of family, occupation and age. We join them at the start of a meeting, just as Tony is bringing the group to order.

Tony Thanks very much for that, Geoff. Welcome everyone – it's good to see you. Rob and Tina send their apologies. Lydia's been poorly, as you know, and it didn't seem right to leave her tonight particularly as we're thinking about being Christian parents. Duncan said he was going to be a bit late, so we'll kick off without him. I've asked Kate to open in prayer.

Kate I just want to read a passage from this week's readings which particularly spoke to me before we begin. It wasn't the verse from Proverbs about a nagging wife being like a dripping tap. That was Sid's favourite. It's the one from Genesis about marriage. It says: 'For this reason, a man will leave his father and mother and be united to his wife and they will become one flesh.' That spoke to me because it tells me that God has a purpose in our marriage and our marriage relationship – for those of us who are married. It gave me a new way of thinking about being a wife. Let us pray. 'Father, thank you that we can be here tonight. We thank you, Lord, that you have called us to know you. And we thank you that you place us in your family, the Church, and that you place us in human families. We pray that tonight you'll help us to share together; that you'll help us to learn from each other and from your word; and that you will bless this meeting. And we pray particularly, Lord, for Lydia and for Rob and Tina as they care for her tonight. In Jesus' name, Amen.'

Tony Thanks, Kate. We're going to be looking this evening, as I said, at how being a Christian affects our family life. As you know, I asked last week if one or two people could just share their own thoughts on this with us. I'm glad to say that this time there was a response. Heather has said she'll begin.

Heather I'm a bit nervous so I've made a few notes. I hope that's OK. As most of you know, I became a Christian just over a year ago and since I started coming to church things have been really difficult for me at home. Peter has given me a very hard time. Looking back, I realize now that I was very depressed before I became a Christian and God has done so much in me. But that's not how it seems to him. At first he just teased me about it. He made jokes about me joining the God Squad and about the people at church. I think he thought it was just a phase and I'd come through it. After all there've been enough phases in my life. He didn't mind me coming to church on the occasional Sunday if we weren't doing anything else. But then I began to come most Sundays. And when I joined Christians for Life I was going out in the evenings as well. I'd never gone to anything without Pete since before we were married. I really wanted him to come with me. Life seemed to be expanding for me in every direction. But he wouldn't come.

Looking back now, I think I went a bit over the top at

first, always nagging him to come to church or come to this or that meeting. We had a furious row the night I was confirmed. It was a wonderful evening and, like the rest of you, I wanted to stand up and say I was a Christian and thank God in public for all he had done for me. When we got home I was riding high, but Pete was furious. He said I'd made him look a fool in front of all those people. It was after that he started making nasty comments whenever he could. He complains that I'm always at meetings. He complains that I love God more than I love him. He says we never get a chance to go out now on Sundays (though we never used to go anywhere anyway). I really want to be able to talk to him about God, but it's become like the forbidden subject between us. I do pray for him. And I do love him. But sometimes it's as though I was torn in two.

Tony Thanks, Heather. Would anyone like to respond to that?

Geoff I shall, if I may, Tony. You all know that Rose became a Christian fourteen years before I did. I took it very badly when she became a Christian. I felt a fool in front of my friends. I was frankly jealous of all these new friends she had, especially the men. I didn't see why she needed God at all. I was very settled in my own life. I didn't need religion, so why should she? At first, like you, she kept nagging me to come to church and come to this meeting and that. Like most men, the more she nagged me, the more determined I was not to come. If I'm honest, I suppose somewhere inside me I was feeling guilty. I wish now that I'd had Rose's courage to find out more about God and stand up for what I believed. But I was too scared of what they would say at work. Sometimes I think it's harder for men.

Heather So how did you come through it?

Geoff I suppose, like everything else in marriage, it was give and take. Rose wanted to do everything at church and be out six nights a week at first. I wasn't having that. We kept rowing, but eventually she got very upset and at long last I saw this really was important to her and wasn't going to go away. So we hit on a compromise. She could go to church once on Sunday and out one night a week. In return, I got to go fishing a bit more in the season. And she agreed to stop trying to get me to church.

Tony How did things change, Geoff?

Geoff Rose tells me now that she stopped nagging and started praying. And it took fourteen years. During that time I think we hardly ever had words on the subject. I stopped being jealous as I gradually got to know people at the church. And then eventually, as you know, God began speaking to me too, partly through Mary's illness. And here I am. Telling Rose I wanted to become a Christian was one of the hardest things I ever did. I had to come at it sideways. I think I would say to you, Heather – don't try and nag Peter into Christianity. You'll never do it. And be sensitive to how he's feeling about it. But don't compromise your beliefs either. I thank God most days that Rose stuck at it despite the opposition. Otherwise I wouldn't be a Christian at all.

Kate You need to pray, love, as well. Just keep praying for him. We'll do the same.

Tony Thanks, Geoff. Thanks, Kate. Michael has kindly offered to share something as well. Over to you, Michael.

Michael shares a very moving and personal account of how he came to Christ when his marriage was on the point of breaking down. For six years he had neglected his wife and two young children in order to build a career. Time away from home led to an affair. Just in time, Michael found Christ. His wife became a Christian as well. By God's grace she was able to forgive. Slowly trust has begun to grow again. Michael knows that he has failed his wife and his children in a very deep way. Uppermost in his mind is the heartfelt desire to make the most of these next years and to be a good Christian husband and father. 'The only trouble is,' he says as he ends his story, 'Work may not be such a pull any more – but there's so much I want to do for God that sometimes I feel a conflict even between God and the family.'

'I think everyone does to some extent', says Tony. 'We all need to come to a balance in the way we use the time we have. In your case, Michael, it really is vital that you give priority time to your wife and children. Don't forget that God has called you to be a husband and father and that's a much more vital calling certainly than anything you might be asked to do in the church.'

Michael But God's done so much for me, Tony. There's an awful lot I want to give back to him now.

Tony I can understand that, Michael. But remember that serving God isn't limited just to the things you do in church. Serving God includes being a good husband or wife, parent, son or daughter. God is not honoured by people who take on too much to the neglect of their family relationships. Sometimes, like spending too much time at work, it can be a form of escapism. We run away from relationships that are not working out at home into the things we do for God at church.

Sid I certainly know what you mean by that, Tony. When I was first a Christian I wanted to be at everything. Two services on Sundays, fellowship during the week; if help was needed I was there. In the end it was just too much.

Michael So how did you decide on the really important things, Sid?

Sid I talked it through with Tony here. He didn't know it at the time, but it was a real help the way he listened. We separated the things that are really essential from the things that are optional. Worship on Sundays is vital for me. Every week, not just when it's convenient. I generally make it in the mornings and sometimes at night if I can. This group is important to me, so Kate and I try not to miss. Beyond that, I do what I can. If someone asks me to help with something I think and pray about it carefully before I say yes. We all lead full lives, so taking something new on means losing time from somewhere else.

Kate Time's something we have to budget, just like money. There's only a limited amount of it. We need to plan in the really essential things, not let them get squeezed out. And one of those essentials is time as a family.

Michael I see what you mean. But what about you, Tony?

You're not married. I suppose that should mean you can give more time to church things, doesn't it?

Tony I thought so at one time, Michael. Like Sid, I went a bit overboard at first as well. But life became very unbalanced. Friends are very important to me. The vicar asked me to take on the youth work a few years ago, but I had to give it up in the end. I just didn't have time after work to keep up with friends and do the youth work justice. Life was slowly shrinking, and I began to realize that all my significant relationships were with Christians.

Heather So will you try and marry a Christian, Tony?

Tony I don't really know whether I want to get married at all, Heather. It's never seemed the right time so far. But I think the answer to your question would be yes. If I did get married I would want my wife to be a Christian. God is so central to my life now, and I don't think it would be acting rightly by God or a prospective partner if we didn't have a common understanding. Do you see what I mean?

Heather No – I mean yes, sorry. I hope you didn't mind my asking.

Tony Not at all, Heather. Everybody else has been sharing quite personal things. Why shouldn't I? I think, if you don't mind though, we'll move to some Bible study now. The passage I'd like us to look at this evening is 1 Corinthians 7. The Christians Paul was writing to in this letter were fairly new to the faith, just like us. Like us, they didn't always get things right and they didn't always agree with each other. Paul was away teaching and preaching somewhere else.

So these new Christians decided to write him a letter and make a list of questions they wanted him to answer. Parts of 1 Corinthians are Paul's answer to that letter. If you look at Chapter 7, verse 1 Paul begins, 'Now concerning the matters you wrote about. . .' It's quite a long chapter so I'm going to divide you up into pairs with each pair looking at a different section. For each section see if you can work out what questions or situations Paul is addressing and whether you think his reply holds good for us today. Just one word of caution before you start. When Paul wrote less than a generation had passed since the resurrection of Jesus and his promise that he would return. The prospect of Jesus' return was a very immediate one for the New Testament church. For that reason, Paul's teaching has an immediacy and urgency to it which we don't often find today. You may like to think about whether our different situation changes how we should apply this chapter.

The group breaks into pairs for shared Bible study and then each pair share their own exegesis of the passage. Tony and the others respond at the end of each section. The discussion ranges over sex in marriage, single people and sexual desires, those whose partners are not yet Christians, and the call to the single life lived for God. There is so much in the chapter that Tony stops the discussion at 9.45 p.m. and saves the rest of the study until next week, disrupting the planned programme, but allowing the group to stay where it wants to be and Rob and Tina to be present. In part two the Bible study will focus on potential conflict between what God wants and what our marriage partner wants; conduct for those who are engaged and right conduct for those who are widowed and (although it is not in the chapter) divorced.

Tony ends the first evening with a short time of worship and a meditation based on 1 Corinthians 13 followed by a very moving time of open prayer. Several of the group lay hands on Heather and pray for her and Peter's marriage. The evening draws to a close with coffee and a short look at the table of books and videos on marriage and family life which Tony has provided. There are also details of a number of courses coming up in the next few months in the church on marriage enrichment and parenting, which is where several people appear to need help at the moment. Everyone thanks Tony very warmly for an excellent evening and departs.

Faith at work

Two weeks later and this time the meeting has started with a Bible study. This time Tony has presented a selection of verses from Proverbs which relate to the theme of work. The group are all comfortable reading aloud and so each person takes it in turn to read a verse and then Tony (and anyone who wants to chip in) comments on it. A time of sharing follows the Bible study. Three members of the group have been asked to comment on an aspect of faith at work. Rob begins with the difficult subject of witness.

Rob Before I begin, Tina and I would like to thank you for your prayers for Lydia and the card you sent. As you know, she's much better. So thanks.

You all know that I didn't become a Christian through church, like most of you. For me it happened through going to hear a speaker at another church in the next town. It was all very sudden. I went forward at the meeting and talked to a man from the church afterwards. I prayed and asked the Lord into my life, and he came. Then the man gave me some advice which was well meant but which backfired. He told me to go and tell someone in the next twenty-four hours that I had asked Jesus into my life.

The most obvious person to tell was Tina, but somehow I couldn't do that. I didn't know any vicars or ministers. So over the coffee break at work I told the rest of the lads on the shift. Just came out with it. 'What did you do over the weekend?' 'Oh, I became a Christian.' 'You what?' At first they were just gobsmacked. Then the mocking began. Pictures of me with a halo on the noticeboard. Graffiti in the toilets. 'Joined the God Squad, have you?' Every shift, every day for weeks on end. It was a baptism of fire really and it nearly finished off the little bit of faith I had. If it hadn't been for Tina and, by then, the folks at this church, I would have given up altogether. It was a misguided attempt to help me become a witness at work from day one. What happened was that it spoiled any chance of my Christian faith being taken seriously.

Tony Did it ease off at all, Rob?

Rob Eventually it did but it still flares up now and again. Every time Cliff Richards is on the telly or another naughty vicar appears in the paper and every time I do something wrong. I'm a bit more hardened to it now and I hope my faith is stronger. But I still don't have much an idea of how to witness at work.

A period of open discussion follows Rob's story. Most of the group feel the same way. Sharing faith at work is difficult. Tony's advice is, in this as in most things, to take things very slowly and prayerfully. Don't compromise. But don't stick your neck out until you are sure it's the right time.

Duncan Can I share what I was going to say now, Tony?

Tony Thanks, Duncan. Go ahead.

Duncan For me, witnessing at work doesn't mean talking about Jesus and church. For me witness at work has meant trying to live out my faith on Mondays as well as Sundays. It wasn't always like that. For quite a while my Christian faith was just for home and Sundays really. I manage a section at work. Sometimes I would go to church on Sunday and be nice and smile at everyone and then go in on Monday morning and treat people as objects, just like I'd done for twenty years. If the job wasn't done right or if it was late, then I'd fly off the handle. I knew people were scared of me, but it was the only way I knew how to get the job done.

Heather My dad used to work at your place. He was amazed when he found out you'd started coming to church.

Duncan That was just the point, Heather. Nobody at work even knew that I came to church or had become a Christian. I didn't advertise it. And nor did the way I behaved.

Kate So how did things change, Duncan?

Duncan Remember that time last year when the clergy had this thing about coming to see people at work? Derek, the curate, asked if he could come and visit the factory. I nearly had a fit. But it was just what I needed. I put him off for a month and said we were really busy just now. Then, very slowly, I began to make some changes. God began speaking to me about the way I behaved at work. My language wasn't too bad. It was more my attitude to people and that temper. One of the hardest things I did was to buy a fish badge and start wearing it at work. I found one of those Christian posters and stuck it on the wall.

Heather How did that make a difference then?

Duncan It was like I was taking God to work with me instead of leaving him at home. Once I'd made a stand and declared I was a Christian, then I began to try and live like one at work too. People noticed. I got some stick. I think they were worried at first that I was going to try and convert them. No one's asked me about it directly. But people do say that they've noticed a change. I'm starting to see people as real individuals now, not just things for getting a job done. I do lose my temper, but I've been known to apologize afterwards now. And another thing, everyone on the section works together. The fear's beginning to go.

Sid So what happened when Derek came?

Duncan That's the funny thing. He never came back to me. The clergy changed their mind and moved on to something else, as they do. But just the threat was enough to make me do something!

Carol It makes you think, though, doesn't it. We worry about someone from church seeing us as we are at work, but God's there all the time. He knows what we're like.

Tony Carol, do you want to share what you had to say?

Carol Thanks, Tony. Mine's a much deeper problem. I don't know if anyone can help me with this, but it would be a relief to share it. You all know I work on the maternity wards as a midwife. Most of the time it's all right. I enjoy what I do. But from time to time I become involved in terminations. . .

Heather Terminations – what, like abortions?

Carol Yes, that's exactly what I mean.

Heather How can a Christian do that?

Carol That's the problem, Heather. It didn't used to bother me before. I swallowed the line all the other professionals use: welfare of the mother and all that. We convince ourselves that what we're doing is really for the best. But that was before I became a Christian. . .

Heather Well can't you just. . .

Tony Heather, can we just let Carol tell her story her way? Thanks. Carry on, Carol.

Carol Thanks, Tony. That's OK, Heather. I know it's a difficult subject. It's just not that simple. I'm in the process of looking for another job but there aren't that many around. And it's not just the fact that I'm involved that upsets me. For the most part I'm involved with caring for the mother anyway. It's not as though I'm involved in the operation. But it's the fact that it happens. Some women just use it like a late contraceptive. Others really want to have their babies and regret it later. It's the whole thing that's wrong and I just don't know what to do.

Kate Have you thought about joining Life, Tina. They would be good people to talk to. . .

The discussion continues around the theme of practical ways Tina can move forward. Eventually Tony brings the group to a close with a time of open prayer. The theme of the prayers is praying for one another at work. Every person shares just one thing for prayer. The group pray especially for Carol in her dilemma and for Geoff who is facing a threat of redundancy. The time of prayer ends with quiet worship and the group say the grace together. Coffee and conversation end the evening.

Study Guide

For Ministers and Church Leaders

Questions for reflection and discussion

1 Look back over your preaching themes for the last two years. How many of the sermon subjects have been relevant to family relationships or to the working environment where people spend most of their lives?

2 What would be the effect of the clergy/pastoral leaders in your church beginning to visit the congregation at work?

3 When people walk into church these days, often they're thinking they'll get the party line again: *Pray more, love more, serve more or give more.*[1] How much of your own preaching has had that theme and how much is geared into helping people where they are?

Ideas for sermons and training courses

1 CPAS have excellent training kits on marriage (*Marriage in Mind*) and parenting (*Help, I'm a Parent*). Both can be used as an excellent base for a course on marriage enrichment or family life.

2 A series of sermons on work issues (honesty, industry, etc) and work dilemmas or perhaps a short series of discussions designed to help equip people to take the Christian faith to work not just in their witness, but in the way they do their job.

3 Visiting people at work and really doing it!

TRACK TWO

For Group Leaders

This track gives you the single session used by Tony on the family. The second half of the chapter should give you enough material for a second session on work.

FAITH IN THE FAMILY

Sharing together

Ask two of the group members to prepare in advance to say something about how becoming Christians has affected their family situation and family relationships. Give each one five to ten minutes to speak to the meeting. Then allow the group to discuss each situation in turn, drawing out lessons from the experience of other group members. Allow the discussion to run as long as it is fruitful.

Bible study

Divide your group into twos and ask them to look at one section of 1 Corinthians 7 on relationships. You will need to divide the chapter up into sections depending on the overall size of the group. Give people about ten minutes in pairs then draw the group together.

Each pair should now share what they have learned from the passage with the rest of the group. Use this sharing for a general discussion about the issues raised and as an opportunity to give any teaching which may be needed.

Prayer exercise

One of the group leads a prepared meditation on 1 Corinthians 13 about Christian love in the family.

After the silence a short time of open prayer follows.

TRACK THREE

For Those Working One-to-One

Again, I suggest you plan two sessions to work through the material in this chapter, not just one. It's difficult to specify here what you will talk about because every person's family and work situation will be different.

In the first session you will be basically talking through the question:
How does my Christian faith affect my family life?

In the second, looking at the question
How does my Christian faith affect my working life?

Introduce Bible study and prayer as seems right. The passages below may give you some ideas.

For Those Working on Their Own

Daily Bible readings

Mon: *Ephesians 5:22–6:4*
Tue: *Colossians 3*
Wed: *Titus 2*
Thurs: *Proverbs 6:1–11*
Fri: *Proverbs 11:1–14*
Sat: *Proverbs 15:1–19*
Sun: *1 Corinthians 13*

Longer exercise

Look back over the time since you became a Christian and record in your journal the different changes that have come about in first your family life and second your working life.

Ask the Lord to show you where he still wants you to change and be changed and make some resolutions together.

NOTES

1 *Mastering Contemporary Preaching*, Bill Hybels, IVP, 1989, p. 37.

twelve

Building a Ministry

Jesus does not call us to be passive spectators in his Church, but active participants. A vital part of growing to Christian maturity is for every Christian to begin to develop a ministry and make a contribution to what is happening. For every person the journey to this ministry will be a slightly different one. By definition, if a person has not yet reached maturity as a Christian then their ministry will not be at its most fruitful. However, that does not mean that there will be no fruit at all or that the church should wait three years before involving new Christians in the work of building the kingdom. The opposite is the case. Doing things for God and living out the Christian life is actually the best way to grow. In seeking to help people develop their own ministries, it's been useful to me to draw out the following stages along the way.

(1) Develop some starting points

Just as no one is born again knowing how to pray so no one is born again as a gifted preacher, pastor, worship leader or administrator. Or at any rate if the gifts are there, it takes time to find your feet in the church and find the right place to use them. It's important therefore to find slots in the life of the Body of Christ where people can begin to find their place and make a contribution from an early stage. Some ministries should be rightly reserved for those who have been part of the family for some time. But if you have to be a church member for fifteen years before you are allowed to read a lesson or wash up the coffee cups there is something wrong. My guess is that small churches find it harder to make room for new members to make a contribution than larger churches. Unless the work is growing rapidly, making room for new people to exercise a ministry means established people being prepared to let go.

The kinds of tasks that are good entry points into ministry in church life include reading the lesson in public worship, assisting on one or more rotas (crèche, coffee etc.), helping with practical tasks such as church cleaning or gardening, acting as a steward or welcomer in church services and so on.

My experience is that people very rarely volunteer for tasks or ministries in the life of the church. Eight months ago we actually put a ban on asking for volunteers for this task or that task in the church notices. It seemed at one time as though it was happening every week and almost never produced fruit. People have different reasons for not offering their services voluntarily. Often they will be very modest and diffident about their own gifts. Sometimes they will simply not know about a need or hesitate to come forward in case it is someone else's job. For that reason there needs to be someone in the church with the responsibility of anchoring new Christians into some form of simple ministry and service within the first year of their joining the church. In a smaller church that should probably be the minister. In a larger church the task needs to be delegated to the evangelism-nurture group or growth group leader possibly liaising with a central co-ordinator. It is an important practical point that an invitation to ministry should always come from the person who knows the individual, not from the person in charge of the rota or ministry.

It's a vital task, not only so that the individual Christians come to feel part of the church family but so that the church itself grows in a healthy way. If a new Christian is 'allowed' to sit back and contribute nothing to church life in the first two years of his or her Christian life, then habits of laziness and just taking in will easily build up and affect the whole pattern into the future.

Every couple of years or so in our own church we conduct

a simple ministry audit. That is, we break down our list of church members into four or five categories. The lists remain entirely confidential. In the first category are those who are not involved in any ministry at all at the present time. In the second list are those who are making a contribution at this very basic 'starter' level in tasks which require very little in the way of training or gifts and which most people can do. In the third list are those who have moved on to a more developed ministry and are taking responsibility as part of a team. At this point in ministry (where, hopefully, most people will be involved) real gifts need to be discerned and exercised and training and commitment is required. In the fourth are those who are exercising leadership and are responsible for others in some way. And in the fifth are those who are responsible for leaders. The table gives you some idea of the kinds of tasks in each group. Over the following twelve months our aim is to seek to enable as many people as we can to move on a category and to develop their ministry further. The lists also provide a very helpful tool in the task all church leaders perform on a weekly basis: finding people for this or that job or ministry.

Not involved	Starter level	Part of a team	Leader	A leader of leaders
Examples	*Examples*	*Examples*	*Examples*	*Examples*
Self-explanatory!	Reads lessons. On crèche rota. Helps with coffee. Cleans church.	Steward. Helps lead children's group. Toddler team member. Sings in choir. Home group co-leader.	Lay reader. Home group leader. Worship leader. MU enrolling member. Toddler team leader.	Children's work co-ordinator. Church-warden. Under fives co-ordinator.

Drawing a graph of the numbers involved in each type of ministry will give you some idea of the health of your church and where you need to focus your work in terms of ministry development in the coming year. Not all of that ministry development will consist of spending time with people to convince them they should take on this or that task. A great deal of it will be in structuring the life of the church so that different opportunities for ministry grow as the numbers in the congregation rise. It's no easy task, but a vital one.

(2) Three ministries we all exercise

Many of the gifts and ministries people use will differ. The New Testament clearly teaches in several places that we are all different. However there are three particular areas of responsibility which we all share as members of a church and as part of the body of Christ. Some may be called to exercise one or more of these ministries to a special degree. However every Christian who is seeking to grow to maturity must develop good practice in these three areas, as well as seek to grow in particular gifts.

(a) The ministry of intercession

Each of us is called to pray and to take on a responsibility for supporting others in prayer. Intercession needs to be a part of the life of every Christian. Sometimes that intercession will be as an individual. Often it will be exercised as part of a group or prayer meeting. If new Christians are to play their part in the intercessory life of the church it is vital that they are equipped at some stage for that ministry. This will mean teaching input at Key Stage 2 in the value of intercession.

As with other things, however, much more will be 'caught' from the general attitude to intercession in the church than is 'taught' through formal groups and sessions. It is also extremely helpful if people can be equipped regularly with needs for prayer and encouraged to keep praying by those in leadership in the congregation.[1]

(b) The ministry of giving

All Christians are called to support the work of the church financially. New Christians should be introduced to the grace and gift of giving at an early stage, preferably during the latter stages of an evangelism-nurture group. In our own church we commend tithing to all our church members as a target to aim at, yet we stress that it will take most people several years to reach that target after they have become Christians.

Again, there is usually a progression. Churches sometimes make the mistake of expecting a gigantic leap from new Christians instead of a number of significant steps. In the first few months of their Christian life we try not to speak to people at all about money. It's much more important that they learn how to receive than how to give. Towards the end of Christians for Life we introduce the subject and encourage people to make an initial transition from 'casual giving' to 'responsible giving'. 'Casual giving' means that I give the loose change in my pocket when the offertory comes round and when I happen to be in church that Sunday. It's where the majority of people begin. 'Responsible giving' means that I take my responsibilities as a member of this church seriously and plan my giving. That will mean I think about it in advance and give an amount which is realistic to the need. I also make provision for my giving to continue if, for any reason, I am unable to be in church one Sunday. That will usually mean giving through an envelope scheme or through a standing order at the bank. If I pay income tax, 'responsible giving' also means taking out a deed of covenant.

At some stage during Key Stage 2 people should then be encouraged to move from 'responsible giving' to 'proportional giving': from giving in response to a need to giving in proportion to our income. It is at this point that some in-depth teaching on the reasons for tithing will be helpful. The initial proportion people decide to give will vary from family to family according to circumstances. Certainly each person needs to come to their own decision before God. Any church policy can only be a guide. Hopefully once people have moved to 'proportional giving', as God continues to work in their lives, the proportion given away will grow according to income in the years ahead.

(c) The ministry of witness

A helpful distinction is often made between being a witness and being an evangelist. An evangelist is someone who is frequently used to draw people nearer to Christ and usually someone who finds it fairly easy to speak of him. Not everyone has that gift. We made a mistake in our church a few years ago when we tried to encourage all those in home groups to undergo an evangelism training programme. Some enjoyed it but those who were not gifted as evangelists really struggled.

However, although we may not all be evangelists, we are all called to be witnesses. Being a witness means two things. It means first that the way we live our lives is consistent with Christ's teaching and speaks of him. Secondly, that we should be prepared to speak in a limited way when someone questions us or asks about what we believe. In the words of 1 Peter: 'Always be prepared to give an answer to everyone who asks you to give the reason for the hope that is in you. . .'[2] In a nutshell, an evangelist makes opportunities to share the faith; a witness takes opportunities that are given. We all need to share in the ministry of witness.

Enabling people to do that is not too difficult so long as new Christians are well grounded in the basics of the faith and confident in speaking with others about what they believe. The encouragement and experience in talking about deep things in small group contexts is a very valuable preparation for this kind of witness. Learning how to tell the story of the way you became a Christian and also how to witness to what God is doing in your life now are both very helpful things to think through in a group.

(3) Developing the right attitudes

When Jesus wanted to demonstrate the central truth of Christian ministry to his disciples he did not give them a lecture or a book to read. He took a towel and a basin of water, wrapped the towel around his waist and went around the room to each person in turn washing feet. To be a Christian minister in any sense is to be a servant. Every congregation has at least some Christians who live out this truth in a very deep way. You will find them, perhaps, emptying the dustbins and changing toilet rolls or doing ironing or cleaning for other families unseen and unnoticed. Some new Christians find that being like a servant in every dimension of Christian ministry comes very naturally to them. But others find just the opposite and are seeking to push themselves to the front and into the limelight at every opportunity.

It's very tempting for those in church leadership to give in to the pressure and allow people who push themselves forward to do exactly what they would like to do. Offers of help may not be that plentiful. We may be subject to unpleasant pressure if the offer of 'service' is not taken up. People may even threaten to leave the church if their 'gifts' are not used. Yet despite all this it is my view, tested through experience, that any ministry which is not offered with the prime motive of being a servant will backfire and will not bear fruit for the kingdom. That means I have learned to be very careful when people say to me in the first few months of their Christian life 'I feel called and/or gifted in this or that area of Christian ministry', particularly if the ministry they are called to involves being seen by others. It is a much better sign of grace when, if people are asked to do something, their response is one of surprise: 'What, me? I could never do that!' We are not called to lord over and exercise control over one another, as is the way of the world[3] but to serve one another. Building a ministry is not about building a kingdom or a power base for ourselves but about building the kingdom of God.

(4) Developing a ministry

Once a person has been a Christian for a year or so,[4] has become settled and established in the basics of the faith, has good disciplines of worship and prayer, has begun to make a contribution in one or more of the 'starting points' described above and has perhaps had a go in a few different areas of church life, then it's time to begin the next stage of development. At this point it is worth the minister or group leader investing some time in exploring what kind of ministry is right for particular individuals and starting them off in particular directions. In one sense shaping and developing a ministry happens over the whole of a person's Christian life. What takes place in Key Stage 2 is just a beginning.

I have found the following questions are a useful guide to work through in conversations with and prayer for people who are developing a ministry.

(a) Should the person's main ministry be inside or outside the church?

It's an obvious point but it needs stating. Not all ministry is exercised within a church. Yes, most people need to be able to make a contribution in some form of service to the life of the local church. But for many people their main area of ministry will be in their workplace, in the family or in some form of voluntary work in the community. We need to be very careful here. The needs of a growing church for more people to do more things can very easily draw energy and life from church members instead of equipping them for service in the world. There does need to be freedom in the life of the church for the primary school teacher or nurse or manager to see their main ministry for God as taking place in the workplace. This should not be seen in any sense as a second-class kind of Christian service. Recent Christian thinking has emphasized 'every member ministry' and there has been a lot written about equipping lay people for ministry in the life of the church, but not so much about equipping people to minister through their work or in the wider community.

(b) How much time is available?

Again, it's an important question. People do have God-given calls on their lives apart from any ministry they undertake within the congregation. For most people, their ministry will be spare time. That means they will be in full-time work in one way or another and the time they have to give is a few hours each week in the evenings and at weekends. In working out possibilities for ministry with people it's important to be realistic about this. For almost everyone in this position it is far more satisfactory to take on one area of ministry over a number of years and do it well than to take on a number of things (or flit from task to task) and do it badly.

Partly because of changing work patterns, an increasing number of people have more time to give and ministry can more honestly be described as part-time. A person may take early retirement from work and be able to make a very significant contribution to one or other area of church life in their retirement years. Our church treasurer and the two men who have managed and directed our building projects fall into this category. So do several of those who staff our church office. Mums with pre-school children are sometimes at home during the day and have time and energy to give to running (for example) parent and toddler groups and for pastoral work.

Sometimes a person will be called by God to work fewer hours (part-time when it could be whole-time) in order to give a significant amount of their working week to ministry in one form or another. Like St Paul, these people are tent makers, using part of their time to earn their living and the rest in Christian ministry. St George's has a pastoral team of six people, two for each congregation. Five out of the six work part time specifically so that they can give a significant part of the rest of the week to ministry. People who are made redundant and, sadly, face a six-month to a year period of not working are also led, on occasions, to offer their time in ministry. The kind of project people in this category can be involved in will obviously be different and more short-term, but the time given can be extremely valuable in building the kingdom.

Finally, a small but very significant group of people will be called to full-time ministry as volunteers. St George's has been extremely blessed over the past four years by the full-time ministry of our administrator and pastoral assistant, both of whom give a full working week to God's service. For that period of time both Catherine and Barbara have been part of the staff team and have worked closely and daily with the clergy.

(c) Is there a call or a burden for a particular area?

Some people have a burden and call for childrens' work. Others are really hungry to see others come to know God. Still others again have a deep desire to worship and help others to worship God or to work with the elderly or disadvantaged, with men, with women or with teenagers. Where there is this clear burden from God, providing a person also has the right gifts and attitude to ministry, it's not too difficult to discern the right direction. Where there is no clear leaning one way or another then you need to move onto the next question!

(d) What gifts does the person have?

Paul calls each of us to minister according to the different gifts and qualities we have been given.[5] Therefore, in helping a person to develop their ministry it's good to have some understanding of what gifts they have, both natural and spiritual. A person gifted in working with children ought normally to think in terms of developing a ministry in that area of the church's life. The person who is good at organization and administration should develop their gifts and ministry there. The person who is good at relating to people should follow a pastoral direction and the person who is good at sharing their faith needs to develop evangelistic ministry. Generally speaking, the more people can be encouraged to specialize and develop their own ministries the more the church can move forward.

Once these four questions have been answered then some picture or pattern for future ministry should be emerging. It may then be possible to slot the person in to a suitable position within the life of the church. Or else some training or preparation may be needed. Or there may not be any 'vacancies' in that particular area at the moment and it may be necessary to wait until new opportunities for ministry develop. Where people begin to be assigned to tasks and responsibilities it is very important that clear guidance, preparation and support are given.[6]

(5) Growing in the gifts of the Holy Spirit

Growing in the gifts of the Spirit is different from developing a particular ministry. Whatever ministry we are called to exercise, the gifts of the Holy Spirit are essential. However, different members of any ministry team will exercise and be given different gifts.

The place for people to begin to exercise spiritual gifts and learn to use them in a mature way is within the small group in the life of the church. It is here that the use of gifts of prophecy, words of knowledge and healing can be modelled and people can be encouraged to step out in faith in a safe environment. Whatever ministry a person is then involved in and committed to, the gifts of the Holy Spirit will enhance and develop that ministry.[7]

(6) Guidance for life

We end where we began. Following Jesus takes a lifetime. As people move through Key Stage 2 and into Key Stage 3 their questions will, hopefully, change from developing a ministry to developing a vocation, from 'What does God want me to do with my time?' to 'What does God want me to do with my life?' Again, as with working out a ministry, it takes time and prayer and patience to assist someone in understanding and discerning their vocation. Growing to maturity means discerning where God wants me to be and following him to that place. The subject is too large to be dealt with adequately here and belongs more properly to a discussion of the Christian journey in the third key stage.

And finally. . . The last great city-wide mission Paul conducted was in Ephesus, the important sea port in Asia Minor. During his mission there was a great revival. Many signs and wonders were seen. Paul gave all he had in teaching and building up the church to maturity during the years he was in Ephesus, not striving to make converts only but to build disciples. In his farewell speech to the Ephesian elders, men and women he himself led to Christ and trained in the Christian way, he looks back on his ministry in the city of building mature Christians, a task to which he gave three years of his life (Acts 20.17–38).

The picture is of a ministry characterized by hard work and by tears (vv. 19, 31) as well as by a deep love of God and for the church. It was a ministry in which he did not hesitate 'to preach anything that would be helpful to you'; a ministry which involved teaching in public from house to house (v. 20).

Paul's charge to the Ephesian elders is to continue this pattern and this model of ministry of making disciples. It is one of the highest callings a man or woman can encounter, to be involved and to share in the pastoral ministry:

Keep watch over yourselves and all the flock over which the Holy Spirit has made you overseers. Be shepherds of the Church of God which he bought with his own blood (Acts 20.28)

May God give to each of us his grace for this ministry.

Study Guide

TRACK ONE

For Ministers and Church Leaders

Questions for reflection and discussion

1 How easy is it for new Christians to find a starting point for ministry within your own church?
2 Conduct a ministry audit as described above. What lessons do you learn about your own situation?

Ideas for sermons and training courses

1 Teaching about the Body of Christ and 'every member ministry'.
2 A sermon series on being a Christian at work.
3 A mini-conference on moving on in the gifts of the Holy Spirit.

For further reading

See the books by John Finney and David Pytches referred to in the notes below.

TRACK TWO
_____

For Group Leaders

The material in this chapter would be extremely difficult to cover in a single session. One possibility would be to develop it into a new series of material on ministry for your group with sessions on (for example):

'Every member ministry'
Intercession
Giving
Witness
Discovering your ministry
Growing in the gifts of the Spirit (a whole series in itself)
Discovering your vocation

The following outline is provided for the sake of completeness and to give you one of the sessions suggested:

_____
DISCOVERING YOUR MINISTRY
_____

Sharing together

Share in twos and threes about the way you have begun to exercise a ministry for God both inside and outside the church since you became a Christian. Pool the groups' answers on a flip chart. In what ways has exercising a ministry helped you to grow?

Bible study

Look together at Romans 12:3–7. Talk about the importance of thinking of ourselves with sober judgement and at the ways God gives different gifts to different people. Give some teaching here about the importance of ministry outside the church.

The four questions

Divide people into pairs and ask them to work through the four questions, answering them for themselves and for their partner. To sum up, go round the group and ask each person to say what kind of ministry they think their partner should be developing. See if the partner and the rest of the group agree.

Prayer exercise

A meditation on John 13:1–17.

For Those Working One-to-One

Again, here are a number of possibilities here as you work through the material in the chapter and plan for future sessions.

As a starter, work through the four questions in the chapter together and discuss areas for possible involvement and ministry inside and outside the church family.

For Bible study look at 1 Corinthians 12:12–31.

For Those Working on Their Own

Daily Bible readings

Mon: *John 13:1–17*
Tue: *Luke 22:24–27*
Wed: *Romans 12:1–8*

Thurs: *1 Corinthians 12:1–31*
Fri: *Ephesians 4:1–16*
Sat: *Acts 20:17–24*
Sun: *Acts 20:25–38*

Longer exercise

Do a self-ministry audit in your journal. Begin by asking the four questions outlined above. Ask God what ministry he wants you to undertake in this next period of your life and listen for the answer over the next few weeks.

NOTES

1 See *Growing New Christians* pp. 35–37 for ten ideas for building prayer in a church.
2 1 Peter 3:15
3 Luke 2:24–27
4 For some people this 'settling down' will take a lot longer depending on their circumstances when they become Christians. In my view it should not be any shorter. I am very hesitant when I hear of schemes for nurture and discipleship where people are thrown in and involved in significant Christian ministry right at the start of their Christian lives.
5 Romans 12:6–7
6 For helpful advice on drawing up job descriptions, handing tasks on, etc. see John Finney, *Understanding Leadership*, Darton, Longman & Todd, 1989.
7 There are a number of helpful books on developing spiritual gifts, particularly David Pytches' *Come Holy Spirit*, Hodder and Stoughton, 1985.

Very helpful
notes under Discipleship